Exploring Summer

Also by Sandra Markle

Exploring Winter

EXPLORING SUMMER

Sandra Markle

*illustrated with drawings and computer graphics
by the author*

Atheneum   1987   New York

Atheneum
Macmillan Publishing Company
866 Third Avenue, New York, NY 10022

Type set by Linoprint Composition, New York City
Printed and bound by Fairfield Graphics, Fairfield, Pennsylvania
Typography by Mary Ahern
Layouts by Susan Lu
First Edition

10   9   8   7   6   5   4   3   2   1

Library of Congress Cataloging-in-Publication Data

Markle, Sandra.   Exploring summer.

Includes index.
SUMMARY: A collection of summertime activities which includes
stories, facts, handicraft, and games.
1. Summer—Juvenile literature.   2. Amusements—Juvenile
literature.   [1. Summer.   2. Amusements]   I. Title.
QH81.M266   1987   790.1'922   86-17322
ISBN 0-689-31212-1

For Frieda and Harry Sauler
and
Bessie and Edward Haldeman,
my grandparents,
who made exploring summer
especially fun.

CONTENTS

IS IT SUMMER YET?

IS IT summer yet? Does the sun slip under your window shade to wake you up in the morning and stick around until way after supper? When you go outside, do you get sunburned cheeks, more freckles on your nose, sweaty feet?

Summer runs down your back and makes your shirt stick between your shoulder blades. It's flowers buzzing with bees, dust swirling along the curb, rainbows hovering in the mist of sprinklers spraying parks and lawns. Summer is cool grass springy under your bare feet, oily suntan lotion, sand gritty inside your wet bathing suit. It's mosquito bites puffing up into red, itchy welts you just have to scratch.

Summer is no homework, baseball, fireworks, hot dogs on a stick roasting over a campfire. It's feeling good wet and chasing fireflies after dark. Summer is bright, thirsty, colorful, exciting.

Is it summer yet? Almost? Then this book is for you.

It has sunny investigations and instructions for building your own solar cooker. There are stories about how animals beat the heat and tales of famous explorers in hot places. It has survival facts and hints for exploring this warm frontier on your own. There are directions for planting a garden that will tell you what time it is and instructions on how to save fruits and vegetables for the winter. You can cook up natural dyes to color a T-shirt and weave a belt on your fingers. There are games to play, riddles to laugh at, and puzzlers to think about. Not to mention indoor explorations for times when it's too awful to go outside.

This book is guaranteed to bring out that secret desire to become an explorer that lurks inside you.

Is it summer yet? Get ready. Summer is too action-packed to miss.

1.
SUMMER
IS COMING

The Secret Of Summer

YOU DON'T want to miss a minute of this season, and you can be ready for it if you watch for the signs. Even if you live where the weather doesn't make a dramatic change, you'll start to see lots of little clues. Bare trees will leaf out, and plants that never lost their leaves will sprout new growth. Flowers will bloom, and birds—familiar feathered friends that haven't been around all winter—will be back. If you really keep your eyes open, you'll see all kinds of animal babies, because summer is a good season for young animals to grow up. However, even surer signs than these are:

1. The constellations you see at night will start to change.
2. It will be daylight longer.

These facts reveal the reason for summer. This season happens because the earth is tilted and because it's orbiting the sun. To find out the secret of how this causes summer, try this investigation. Stick a toothpick through the center of a marshmallow. Then, hold the pick near the top and keep it pointing straight up and down while you move the marshmallow in a slow orbit around a glowing lightbulb. Notice how both the upper and the lower half of the marshmallow are brightly lit during the complete trip. If this model represented the way the earth orbits the sun, winter and summer would be just alike.

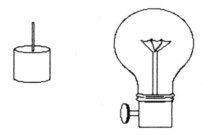

In fact, that's the way it is at the equator—hot and sunny all the time. However, to make the model simulate the earth's real position, you'll need to tip the marshmallow so the top end of the pick points away from the bulb. Keep it tilted while you repeat the orbit and watch closely. Through part of its course, the lower half of the marshmallow receives more direct light. Then, the marshmallow moves to a position where the top half is aimed at the lightbulb. Whichever of the earth's hemispheres—northern or southern—is receiving direct radiation from the sun has summer.

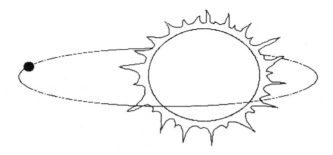

The earth takes 365¼ days to complete one orbit of the sun, and during that time the earth's position in space is constantly changing. Because of the earth's tilt, this orbital shift is enough to make the angle at which the sun's rays strike the earth a little different each day. It also makes the sun rise and set in a slightly different place on the horizon. Twice during each orbit, the sun rises exactly due east and sets exactly due west. Those two days are called the vernal (spring) equinox and the autumnal (fall) equinox. These days are called equinoxes because the hours of daylight and darkness are equal. Orbit the tipped marshmallow again. Can you find the two points when the effect of the tilt is the least—the equinoxes?

After the spring equinox, the sun rises a little to the north of east each day and sets a little to the south of west. The more to the north the sun rises, the greater the arc it traces across the sky before setting. This means more hours of daylight—more hours of direct solar energy to heat up the earth. Although the days are warm long before this official date, summer begins in the northern hemisphere on June 21. That's the summer solstice, the longest day of the year, when the earth's North Pole is pointed most directly toward the sun. Ninety-three days and approximately fifteen hours later, summer ends on September 23, the autumnal equinox. If you live in the southern hemisphere, June 21 is the shortest day of the year for you. December 21 is the longest day. Just think—for those who celebrate Christmas south of the equator, this holiday is one of the longest days of the year!

PUZZLER

> *Bees have a special way of communicating called the "bee dance" that uses the sun to give directions to a source of pollen some distance from the hive. How do dancing bees deliver their message?*
>
> *(See page 12.)*

Sun Followers

PREDICTING when it would be summer and tracking the sun's behavior in general was very important to the ancient Egyptians, Greeks, Sumerians, Zunis, and others. These early civilizations valued the importance of the sun to life on earth so much that they made it one of their gods. They built massive stone observatories devoted to studying and worshiping the sun. Stonehenge in England and the avenue of standing stones at Carnac in Brittany show that observers nearly four thousand years ago knew about the sun's precise movements. During the summer solstice, sunlight illuminates a line of key stones at Stonehenge. A temple to the sun god Re (pronounced *ray* and also spelled Ra) that the early Egyptians built at Karnak has a long avenue of columns. The fact that the avenue is illuminated down its entire length on only two days a year isn't chance. Those two days are the vernal and autumnal equinoxes.

The Egyptians depended on the Nile River's annual flood for a fresh deposit of fertile topsoil, and predicting this event was important in order to plant at the right time. After years of careful observations, they learned that the Nile always flooded just after Sirius, the brightest star in the constellation Canis Major, appeared as the last star on the horizon before dawn. While watching for this star, they were also tracking where the sun rose each morning. This led them to develop a solar calendar that was much more accurate for their purposes than a lunar (moon) calendar.

Because Sirius, also called the "dog star," appeared overhead when the long, hot days of summer set in, the uncomfortably warm days of July and August became known as "dog days." The name stuck.

The flat-topped stone temples the ancient Aztecs built in Mexico are wonders of solar astronomy. The stairs stretching up one side have 360 steps—one for each day of their solar calendar. A number of the temples have sections that are illuminated only during the equinoxes or during the solstices. The most famous remaining sculpture left by the Aztecs is their solar calendar, a stone disk nearly 12 feet (3.7 meters) in diameter. The face of Huitzilopochtuli, their sun god, apears at the center, surrounded by carvings representing the days of the Aztec months and religious symbols. This solar calendar was divided into eighteen twenty-day months with five extra days. The calendar was designed to determine the exact date for religious ceremonies. However, knowing it was time to worship the sun wasn't always good news if you were an Aztec. They believed that Huitzilopochtuli needed human hearts and blood to remain strong, and it's thought that these human sacrifices were placed on the calendar stone.

Some of the most fanciful myths about the sun were developed to explain its movement across the sky. The ancient Egyptians believed Re sailed in a boat. The Greeks thought that the sun god drove a chariot through the sky and that the sun was actually one of this vehicle's blazing wheels. In Mesopotamia the sun god Shanash also rode a chariot, but he had a chauffeur to drive him. Shanash supposedly came out of the mountain from the Door of the East and climbed into his waiting chariot. Then, after his ride, he went through the Door of the West and traveled underground to get back to the east before morning. The Maoris in New Zealand explained that the sun took a whole day to cross the sky because it was limping. One of their heroes had fought with and wounded the mighty sun.

Whatever explanation they gave for the sun's daily journey from horizon to horizon, these ancient people used it as a means of telling time.

The oldest sundial found is one that was used by the ancient Egyptians in approximately 1500 B.C. The Incas of Peru used giant granite monuments as sundials. You can build a sundial of your own to investigate how this solar clock works.

You'll need:

> a forked stick
> a straight stick about 3 feet (.9 meters) long
> a compass
> a protractor
> twelve flat stones painted white
> a permanent ink marking pen
> a spot of bare dirt

Push the forked stick into the ground in the middle of the open area. The angle formed by the base of this stick and the ground must be a 90 degree angle—like the angle formed by the corner of a room. Check this angle with the protractor. Then use the compass to determine which way is due north. Turn the forked stick if necessary, so when the straight stick is laid through the fork it points north. Move the straight stick forward or backward until the angle formed where it touches the ground is the same number of degrees as the latitude for the city where you live on earth. You can find your city's latitude in an atlas. For example, if you live in Boston, your latitude is 42 degrees north. In Denver, it's 50 degrees north, and in San Francisco it is 37 degrees north. Use the protractor to check this angle, too.

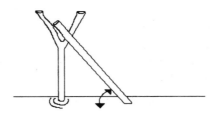

The part of the sundial that will cast the shadow is the pointer you formed with the two sticks. This pointer is called the gnomon (nō′ män). To finish your sundial, check the position of the shadow cast by the gnomon each hour during the day. Mark that position with a white stone and write the number of the hour on the stone with the marking pen.

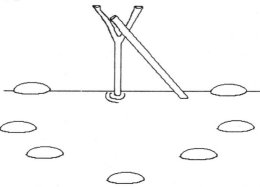

Your summer sundial won't tell time accurately in the winter. Why do you think that's true?

PUZZLER ANSWER

As the bee dances, it makes a short, straight run followed by a circling that forms a figure 8. Scientists have determined that the straight run points out the direction—in relation to the sun's position in the sky—that the other bees should follow. The distance between the extreme ends of the two loops, it's believed, indicates how far away the pollen source is.

RIDDLE

What do you get when you cross a rabbit and a spider?

A harenet.

Sun-Powered Flower

SUNFLOWERS really keep track of the sun. Normally growing from 3 to 10 feet (1 to 3 meters) tall, these plants turn their big flower heads slowly to face the sun throughout the day. A sunflower head is actually a disk of many small tubular flowers surrounded by a fringe of large yellow petals.

Plant some *Helianthus* (a giant variety of sunflower) seeds on the day you get out of school, then watch the action all summer. The seeds should be planted ½ inch (1.25 centimeters) deep and 3 feet (.9 meters) apart in a sunny spot. You may want to measure your tallest plant to see how it compares with the world's record-holder. Frank Killand of Exeter, England, grew the champion sunflower— over 23 feet (7 meters) tall.

When summer's over, the flower petals dry and fall off, and the center turns black. Then you can harvest the seeds. They make a tasty treat. One sunflower head may yield as many as one thousand seeds. Break open the outside shell and eat what's inside. You may want to save some to mix with other seeds and share with the birds next winter.

Animals Get Ready For Summer

AS SUMMER approaches, animals that have hibernated through the winter wake up and become active. Those that migrated—traveled to where it was warmer—head north, returning to where there is less competition for food or instinctively heading for traditional breeding grounds. They compete for mates, build nests, dig burrows, and establish territories. Many animals have babies so the young can grow up during the summer, when food is plentiful and the weather is less challenging. With summer approaching, it's time for new coats and feathers, a change of color, and even—sometimes—a whole new body shape.

Mountain Goats

WHEN the mountain goats start to climb, it's a sure sign that summer is coming. Once the deep snows melt, they quickly leave their winter refuge in canyons and valleys for their high summer range. They often travel above 10,000 feet (3,048 meters) in the Rocky Mountains of Montana and Idaho or in the Cascade Mountains of Washington. Soft,  rubberlike foot pads combined with concave hooves make these animals surefooted mountain climbers. Even the kids, born early in June, are active within a few hours, leaping and bounding along narrow ledges.

American Bison (Buffalo)

WHEN warm weather arrives, the buffalo begin to shed. They'll rub against anything rough to help scrape off their heavy winter coats. As the summer grows hot, the buffalo keep on rubbing— this time to ease the discomfort of insect bites. Determined scratchers have been known to rub until poles, fence posts, or road signs fall over. Buffalo territory is marked with deep troughs where the big animals paw up the dirt and wallow in the dust to soothe their hides. Luckily, bison have fair-weather friends. Magpies and cowbirds perch on their backs, dining on the insects that infest the buffalo's furry coat.

Monarch Butterflies

IN FEBRUARY the monarch butterflies begin to flap their wings in the warm sun. Slowly they become more active. All winter these adults have rested, clinging by the millions to the branches of the trees near Pacific Grove, California. Others wintered in the mountains of Mexico. The monarchs mate.

Then they begin the long trip back—northward. The males soon die, but the females go on, depositing their eggs on milkweed plants. The leaves of this plant are the only food monarch caterpillars eat. The young monarchs develop into butterflies in just three weeks and continue heading north. Eventually the monarchs spread into Canada. Watch for them. When you see these big orange and black butterflies, you'll know summer is just around the corner. They won't head south again until about September. (For more information on this butterfly's life cycle, see page 105.)

Northern Fur Seals

ALTHOUGH they've wandered alone or in small groups all winter, fur seals head for a reunion on the Pribilof Islands as summer nears. The big bulls (males) arrive early in May, fighting each other for a spot, their territory, on the rocky land. It's a good thing the bulls are fat—weighing an average of 420 pounds (190.5 kilograms)—because they won't leave to eat again for about fifty days. The cows (females) arrive a few weeks later and are herded into harems by the bulls. Each

female will have one pup—or, rarely, twins—in June or July. Then the seals mate, beginning the development of a new baby that will be born the following summer. For the next four months, the seals will remain at the rookery while the pups nurse and grow big enough to face a winter in the open sea.

Arctic Hares

CHECK this bunny's coat to know the season. In the winter it's as white as the snow. In the summer the arctic hare is brown like the ground. This camouflage coloration is especially important for the mother hare protecting her young. She doesn't dig a burrow because in the Arctic only the very surface of the ground thaws. Instead, she scrapes a hole for a nest. The young are born furry. They are able to hop about in a day or two and no longer need their mother's milk within two weeks. Arctic hares have to grow up fast because it takes a strong animal to withstand an arctic winter. Luckily, summer days are very long, and there are plenty of juicy plants to eat. Meanwhile, mom will produce two more litters before the first of September—just to be sure some arctic hares survive.

Bald-Faced Hornets

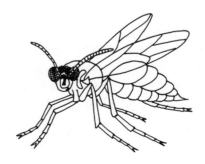

AS SOON AS a hornet queen emerges from hibernation, she choses a sheltered site and begins to build a house. The female hornet is both architect and construction worker. She even supplies the basic building material—paper. To make the paper, she scrapes off thin slices of wood with her sharp mandibles (teeth-like mouth parts) and mixes the pulp with her saliva. Next, she starts her house with a small cluster of egg chambers, each a perfect six-sided cell. Then she covers this cluster with sheets of tough, thick paper. The paper is good enough to write on, but don't try to steal the hornet's siding. Eventually this house will be home to thousands of hornet workers—all able to sting to defend it. While the queen lays more eggs, the workers take over the job of building egg chambers. With each new addition, the hornets' home grows bigger. By summer's end the paper house may be as big as a basketball. Because of the air trapped between the outer protective layers, the inside stays cool as the temperature rises. If it gets too hot, the workers will even carry home droplets of water, wetting the paper. The evaporating water acts like air-conditioning. If you spot a paper house starting on a tree branch or under a house eave now, you can watch the construction all summer long.

Leopard Frogs

HAVE the leopard frog tadpoles sprouted legs yet? Sometime between March and May, when the pond water temperature reached 41°F (5°C), the females laid their eggs while the males spread sperm over them. One female could deposit as many as 4,500 eggs. Eight to twenty days later, the tadpoles hatched. At 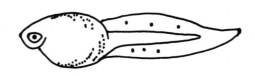 first, each tadpole attached itself to a water plant by two tiny suckers under its head. It stayed there two or three days while its eyes, mouth, and tail formed. Then the tadpole began to swim freely, eating water plants and dead animals. Many tadpoles were eaten—by fish, birds, turtles, large water insects, and even other tadpoles. Those that survived grew bigger. Gradually their external gills were replaced by internal ones, they sprouted hind legs, and their tails shortened. Next, their complete body shape changed, and their gills were replaced by lungs. By summer the tadpoles will be adult leopard frogs, basking in the sun and watching for a tasty insect dinner.

Toad eggs

Frog eggs

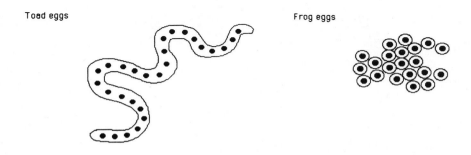

If you find toad or frog eggs, you may want to bring some home to watch their special life cycle. You'll be able to tell whether you're collecting frog eggs or toad eggs by the way they're arranged. Frog eggs are usually in clusters. Most toad eggs are in tubes or strings. Partly fill a self-sealing plastic bag with pond water and then scoop a few eggs into the bag—you won't want to take care of thousands of developing young. Be sure to add some water plants, such as duck-weed. This is the green scum floating on top of the pond. At home, pour your visitors into a small fishbowl or a quart jar.

As soon as you see the tadpoles swimming around, move them to a larger container filled with pond water. Or you can fill the tank with tap water that has been allowed to sit out for several days. You'll also need to keep the tank well stocked with pond plants so the growing tadpoles will have enough to eat. If the natural food supply runs low, add a piece of boiled lettuce. Change the water every few days and keep the tadpoles out of direct sunlight.

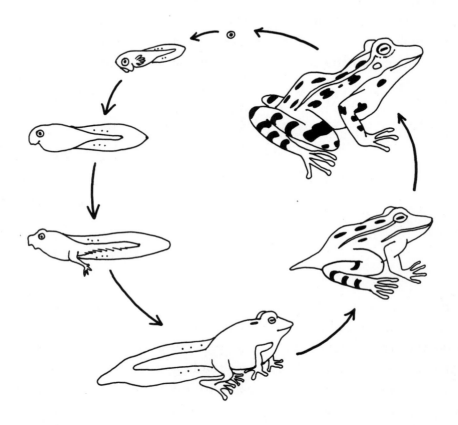

About the time you first see the tadpoles sprout hind legs, you'll need to move them to an aquarium in which rocks and gravel have been piled at one end for the young adult frogs to climb out of the water. At this time you'll also need to cover the top of their home with a piece of screen so the young frogs can't hop out. Now they'll need mealworms and small insects to eat. Adult frogs eat only live prey. So once your guests are mature, be ready to catch a lot of food. Or bid them farewell and take them back to their home pond. Then you can go visit them. Although you may not recognize each other, the frogs you raised can live as long as twenty-five years—if they avoid the many animals that enjoy frogs for dinner.

Dandy Daddies

NOT ALL tadpoles are left to take care of themselves. The male Darwin frog of Argentina guards the eggs during the two to three weeks they take to develop. Then, just before they are ready to hatch, he scoops up the eggs with his tongue and deposits them inside his vocal sac, a huge stretchy pouch that covers his whole belly. Considering that Dad is only 1 inch (2.5 centimeters) long, that's a mouthful. About twelve weeks later, when the tadpoles mature, Dad opens wide, and as many as twenty young frogs hop out, ready to face the world.

Growing Down?

AS YOU MATURE, you'll grow up—meaning that among other changes you'll get bigger. For at least one group of frogs, just the reverse happens, however. Tadpoles of the paradoxical frog, which lives in South America, are about 13 inches (33 centimeters) long. As they change into frogs, they shrink. Adult paradoxical frogs are only about 1.5 inches (3.8 centimeters) long.

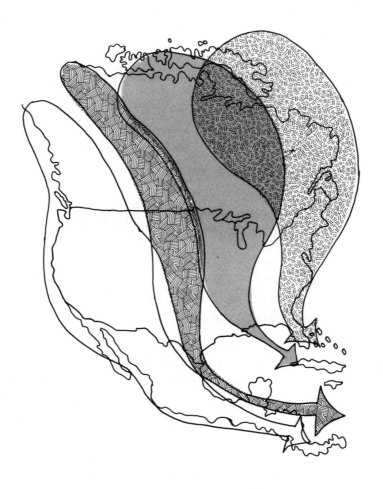

RIDDLE

What happens to ducks when they fly upside down?

They quack up.

On The Road Again

THE MAP on page 22 shows the four main flyways birds follow across North America as they migrate. Ornithologists, people who study birds, believe that many feathered travelers find their way based on the position of the sun. Night fliers use the moon and stars to guide them. If you live close to one of these routes, you'll want to watch for passing flocks. While many birds are limited to a small area during the winter, a plentiful food supply and suitable temperatures allow them to spread out over a much larger range in the summer. The scarlet tanager, for example has a winter range in South America that is only 100 miles (161 kilometers) wide. However, its summer range covers more than 1,900 miles (3,057 kilometers) across Canada and the United States. The following chart shows some of the longest-distance travelers you'll see heading north.

arctic tern	*11,000 miles (17,700 kilometers) from the shores of Antarctica to islands bordering the North Polar Basin and also to Great Britain and to Massachusetts in the United States*
barn swallows	*7,000 miles (11,263 kilometers) from Argentina to Alaska—350 miles (563 kilometers) of that is nonstop over the ocean*

whooping crane	2,500 miles (4,023 kilometers) from Arkansas National Wildlife Refuge in Texas to Wood Buffalo Park in Canada
bristle-thighed curlew	2,000 miles (3,218 kilometers) from the Hawaiian Islands to Alaska

Walking Home

WHEN the mountain quail heads for its summer nesting grounds, it walks. Traveling in small groups, these birds hike as much as 30 miles (48 kilometers) up into the Sierra Nevada Mountains of California. In September the birds troop back down to lower valleys for the winter.

Build a Bird a Home

IF YOU build a house, a bird family may settle in your neighborhood. Here are plans for both a quickie and a more permanent dwelling. If you have tenants, follow the checksheet on page 28 for some interesting summer bird-watching.

House Plan #1. You'll need:

> an opaque (can't see through it) plastic container with a
>   snap-on lid
> three small nails
> a piece of 2 × 4 board about 4 inches (10 centimeters) longer
>   and 4 inches (10 centimeters) wider than the
>   diameter of the lid
> a small wedge of wood
> wood glue
> a ruler
> two long nails
> a hammer
> fine-grained sandpaper
> sharp-pointed scissors

(You may want an adult's help.)

1. Use the three small nails to attach the lid to the center of
   the board.
2. Hold the container so one side becomes the bottom wall.
   Use the scissor points to drill several holes in the bottom
   wall. These will let out any rainwater that might get inside
   the house.
3. Cut a hole 1.5 inches (3.8 centimeters) in diameter in the
   closed end of the container. Position the hole toward the

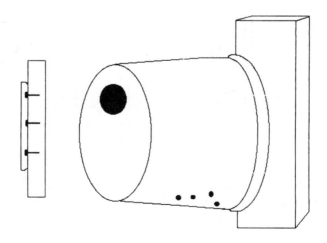

top to let bird residents enter above their nest. Sand the edges of this hole smooth.

4. Use wood glue to attach the wedge to the top rim of the board.

5. Snap the container onto the lid.

House Plan #2. You'll need:

enough ¾-inch (1.9-centimeter) boards to cut each of the pieces shown in the diagram (see measurements below)

a saw

a coping saw

a drill

a hammer

a 4 × 4 inch (10 × 10–centimeter) piece of 1.5-inch (3.75-centimeter) board

about twenty 1.75-inch (4.4-centimeter) galvanized steel or aluminum nails

a wood dowel, .5 × 5.5 inches (1.3 × 14 centimeters)

a 1.5-inch (3.75-centimeter) wood screw

a metal washer

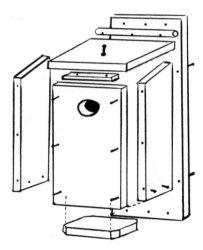

Plans courtesy of The North American Bluebird Society, Inc. For more information, about bluebirds and other cavity-nesting birds, you can write to them at P.O. Box 6295, Silver Spring, MD 20906.

1. Cut the main house pieces: top, 6.5 × 7 inches (16.5 × 17.8 centimeters); front, 5.5 × 9.5 inches (14 × 24.1 centimeters); sides, 4 × 10.75 inches (10 × 27.3 centimeters) along the back edge and 4 × 9.45 inches (10 × 24 centimeters) along the front edge; back, 5.5 × 16.75 inches (14 × 42 centimeters); bottom, 4 × 4 inches (10 × 10 centimeters). Cut off the corners of the bottom for drainage.
2. Drill a guide hole. Then use the coping saw to cut a door 1.5 inches (3.75 centimeters) in diameter in the front.
3. Assemble the house as shown in the picture. Drill holes to start the nails as you attach the pieces.
4. Nail the dowel to the back. Then slide the top under the dowel and drill a hole for the wood screw through the top into the front. Add the screw and washer to hold the top in place.

Mount either of these two birdhouses at least 3 feet (.9 meters) off the ground to help discourage predators. A metal post is even better than a tree because it's harder for the birds' enemies to climb. The doorway size shown is ideal for bluebirds. These beautiful birds aren't as common as they used to be because people have cut down most of the old fence posts and many of the trees that had holes where they could nest. Bluebirds are hard to miss, but if you get another tenant, check a bird book to identify it. Chickadees, swallows, titmice, wrens, and nuthatches are also cavity-nesters, as hole-dwellers are called, and interesting neighbors.

Bird Watcher's Checklist

FIND A QUIET, shady spot where you can get comfortable and observe. If you have binoculars available, use them for a better long-distance view. Try to answer these questions as you watch:

1. What type of birds are living in your birdhouse?
2. Does the male bird look different from the female?
3. What kind of nesting materials do the birds carry in? Who seems to be doing most of the building—the male or female?
4. Can you tell when there are baby birds in the nest? Write down the date.
5. What kind of food do the parents bring for the young? Count how many trips the parents make carrying food to the nest in one hour. Find out how many hours of daylight there are and estimate how many trips the parents make each day.
6. How long before you see the young birds leave?

If you're lucky enough to have bluebirds move in, you can coax them to raise as many as three broods during the summer. As soon as you see the young birds leave, remove the nest. (Wear old gloves when handling the nesting material, and be sure the residents are out. You may want an adult's help with this job.) The parent birds will build a new nest and start another family.

Eating Sunlight

IF YOU sit out in the sunshine, all you'll get is sunburned. Place a green plant in the sunshine, however, and it will make food in the form of a simple sugar. This process is called photosynthesis.

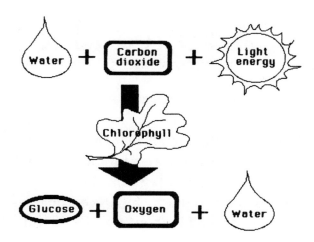

Green plants are the only living things that can produce their own food. They're the beginning of every food chain. When you eat beef, pork, and chicken, you're eating meat from an animal that ate a plant. You also eat a lot of green plants, or seeds and fruits produced by green plants, however. Here's a list to get you started. Can you name at least ten more green plants that produce food for you?

lettuce	celery	Brussels sprouts
cabbage	spinach	kale

Green plants not only produce food during photosynthesis, they also give off oxygen, the gas all animal life needs to breathe in order to survive.

A Potted Plot

I F YOU'D like to grow some plants of your own, you'll need to get started before summer comes. Even if you have a lot of spare land around your home, start small. Plant a potted garden. Collect the gallon-size plastic buckets that ice cream comes in. Use the pointed tip of sharp scissors to bore six to ten drainage holes in the bottom of each one. Then spread about 1 inch (2.5 centimeters) of pebbles or gravel in the bucket and fill it about two-thirds full of potting soil. Mix in one-half to one cup of humus—decaying plant material, such as peat moss. Some soils are better than others for encouraging plant growth. By using potting soil, you don't have to worry about soil quality. Potting soil has been especially prepared to support plant roots, provide adequate drainage, and supply needed minerals. For

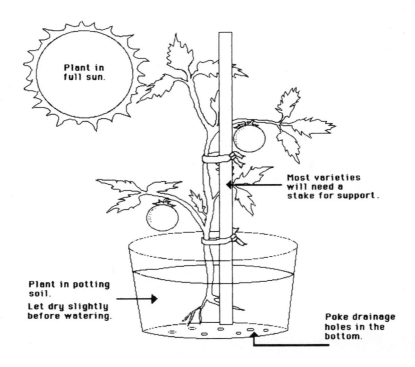

Plant in full sun.

Most varieties will need a stake for support.

Plant in potting soil.
Let dry slightly before watering.

Poke drainage holes in the bottom.

best results, however, it's a good idea to add a commercial fertilizer (following the directions on the package label) about once a week while your garden is growing.

Some good crops to grow in your potted plot are tomatoes, potatoes, radishes, and onions. Because your garden is mobile, you can place each plant where it will get the amount of sunlight it needs each day.

Or you could plant a garden that would tell you what time of day it is. Carl von Linné, more commonly called Linnaeus, developed a special floral garden in Sweden in 1748. At each hour of the day and night, a different type of flower was open. Check in seed catalogs for flowers that bloom at specific times. Here's a list of suggestions and the times they are open based on Eastern Standard Time.

5:00–6:00 A.M.	Dwarf morning glories wild roses pumpkin flowers
7:00–8:00 A.M.	dandelions
8:00–9:00 A.M.	African daisies
9:00–10:00 A.M.	gentians
10:00–11:00 A.M.	tulips California poppies
Noon	goatsbeard chicory stars-of-Bethlehem
4:00 P.M. Sunset	four-o'clocks evening primroses moonflowers
9:00–10:00 P.M.	flowering tobacco
10:00 P.M.–2:00 A.M.	night-blooming cereus

Are the birds busy feeding their babies? Are there bees buzzing around the flowers and caterpillars chewing on the leaves? Is it daylight until late and warm enough by noon to be considered hot?

GREAT!
Summer is here.
Don't wait another minute
to get started.

2.
HOT INVESTI-GATIONS

Straight From The Source

THE SUN is a powerhouse, sending out a whole energy package. There are cosmic rays, gamma rays, X-rays, ultraviolet rays (which cause sunburn), visible light, infrared rays, and radio waves. About 80 percent of the sun's energy that reaches the earth is visible light, about 16 percent is infrared rays, and about 4 percent is ultraviolet rays.

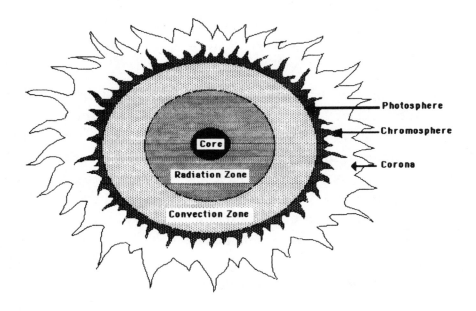

Core: 27,000,000°F (15,000,000°C). Hydrogen changes to helium here. These thermonuclear reactions have the force of millions of atomic bombs.

Radiative zone: 4,500,000°F (2,500,000°C). Energy generated in the core spreads out in all directions.

Convective zone: 2,000,000°F (1,000,000°C). Energy continues to flow outward toward the surface.

Photosphere: 10,000°F (5,500°C). This is the innermost layer of the sun's atmosphere. It appears to be made of many small granules that are caused, astronomers believe, by waves of churning gas in the convective zone.

Chromosphere: 50,000°F (27,800°C). No one's sure why the temperature rises again. Streams of gas called spicules shoot up periodically. Disturbances in the sun's magnetic field can also cause prominences—bright arches of gas—fountains, flares, and sunspots. Sunspots appear as dark patches that seem to move as the sun rotates. Sunspot activity has been observed to occur in cycles, with a maximum number appearing every eleven years.

Corona: 4,000,000°F (2,200,000°C). Halolike, it's only visible during a solar eclipse, when the moon's shadow blocks out the bright photosphere and chromosphere. As the gases continue to expand outward from the corona, they become what is called solar wind.

In the summer the sun's rays strike the earth most directly. This investigation will let you discover why that makes a difference. Fill a quart jar with water and add one-half teaspoon of milk, stirring to mix. The cloudiness simulates the earth's atmosphere, the enveloping blanket of water vapor and gases. Hold a white index card on one side of the jar, as shown in the picture below. Next, hold the flashlight above the water and tilt it so the light must angle down and across the water in the jar. See how spread-out and hazy the light beam appears? The light falling on the card makes only a dim spot. This is the way the sun's rays strike the earth during the winter.

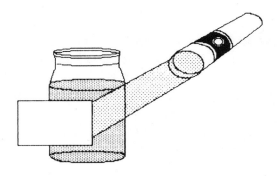

Now direct the flashlight beam straight through the milky water at the card. See how much clearer and more focused the narrow beam appears, slicing through the water? The light makes a bright spot on the card. Like earth in the summer, each square centimeter of the card receives a more concentrated dose of light than it did during the first investigation.

PUZZLER

Why are gaps left between sections of railroad track?

(See page 39.)

What Happens When Something Gets Hot?

ON A DAY when the weatherman is predicting "hot and sunny," set up the investigation shown below.

1. Make a miniature bucket out of a paper cup. Poke holes on opposite sides of the cup with sharp scissors. Thread a piece of string through one hole and knot it. Thread it through the other hole, allowing a little slack in the middle, and knot it. Put paper tape over the knots to strengthen the bucket.

2. Press a large tack into the end of a paint-stirring stick. Lay the stick on a table or chair

seat with the tack sticking out over the end. Use books to anchor the stick.
3. Measure from the stick to the ground and cut a piece of thin copper or aluminum wire that is 6 inches (15 centimeters) longer than that distance.

4. Tie one end of the wire around the tack. Tie the other end to the cup bucket's handle.
5. Half fill the bucket with pebbles.
6. Adjust the wire until the bottom of the cup is 1 inch (2.5 centimeters) above the ground.

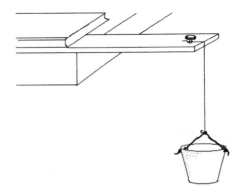

Check every two hours, measuring how far off the ground the bottom of the bucket is. The wire, like all matter, is made up of atoms and groups of atoms called molecules. Because the wire is a solid, these building blocks are tightly packed together. Heat energy makes the atoms and molecules begin to move, bumping into each other and bouncing apart. This movement causes the solid wire to expand. That's why as the day heats up, you'll discover the bucket sinking closer to the ground. How much does the wire expand? If the bucket touches the ground, repeat the experiment on the next hot day. This time start the bucket 2 inches (5 centimeters) off the ground.

While different solids expand different amounts in response to an equal increase in temperature, rubber is an oddball. Repeat the investigation you just completed using a thick rubber band cut to form a single rubber strip. As it grows warmer, the stretched rubber will contract slightly. Skin and leather react this same way.

Measuring Heat

THIS THERMOMETER below shows the hottest temperature ever recorded in Death Valley in California. This is the hottest place in the United States.

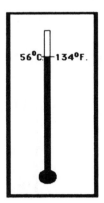

Measuring temperature is always measuring heat—how much or how little of it is present. A thermometer has a small bulb full of colored alcohol or mercury, a metal that is a liquid at normal air temperature, opening into a slender sealed tube. All the air molecules have been removed (forming a vacuum) so there isn't anything to block the tube. As heat energy speeds up molecular movement, the alcohol or mercury expands into the tube. The more heat, the higher the column rises.

Find out how hot it is outside at your house. You'll need an indoor/outdoor thermometer. First, check to see whether your thermometer shows the Fahrenheit (F) or Celsius (C) scale, or both. What is the highest temperature—on each scale if both are shown—on your thermometer? (The symbol for degrees is ° as in 75°F.) What is the lowest temperature? How many degrees does each little line between the major marks on your thermometer represent? Put your thermometer outside in a sunny place. Be sure it's protected from the wind. Wait thirty minutes and check the temperature.

For one day, check and record the temperature every two hours from sunrise to sunset. You may want to use this information to make a line graph of the results. What was the biggest temperature increase? What time of day did it occur? When was it hottest? How much had the temperature dropped by sunset?

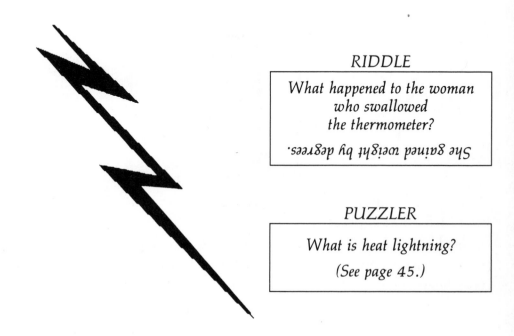

RIDDLE

What happened to the woman who swallowed the thermometer?

She gained weight by degrees.

PUZZLER

What is heat lightning?

(See page 45.)

Light Tricks

ON A HOT DAY, you might see what looks like a pool of water shimmering on a distant stretch of highway or parking lot. Don't plan to jump in. What you're seeing is a mirage. Visible in deserts and at sea, too, this is really an optical illusion. Hot air near the earth's surface is refracting (bending) light rays and bouncing an image of the sky to your eyes.

Refraction also makes the sun appear larger when it's close to the horizon. For a closer look at how refraction fools your eyes, you'll need a penny, clear tape, a cereal bowl, and a pitcher of water (it should be one you can easily hold with one hand). Make a loop of tape and stick the penny to the center of the bottom of the bowl. Hold the bowl at eye level with your nose touching the side. You may just be able to see the penny. Or you may not be able to see the penny at all, but keep looking straight ahead as you begin to pour water into the bowl. (You may want to have a friend pour the water.) As the bowl fills, you'll be able to see more and more of the penny.

Bouncing Heat

SUMMER heats up because of what happens to the sun's energy after it reaches the earth. Infrared rays are heat rays. Like visible light waves, these rays are absorbed and reflected in varying amounts by everything on earth. Set up these three investigations to find the good infrared ray absorbers.

1. You'll need:

> two shoe boxes
> white construction paper
> black construction paper
> glue
> scissors
> two indoor/outdoor thermometers

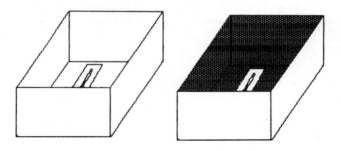

Line one shoe box with white paper and the other with black paper. (Or you could paint the inside of one box white and the other black.) Place the two boxes side by side outdoors in a sunny spot. Be sure they are shielded from the wind. Compare the two thermometer readings. If they aren't exactly the same, record the readings. You'll need to know the starting temperatures to be able to tell how much the temperature changes during the investigation. Lay one thermometer in the bottom of each box. Wait thirty minutes and then check the readings again. Which shows the greatest increase?

2. You'll need:
   two plastic milk jugs
   scissors
   string
   a paper clip
   dirt
   two indoor/outdoor thermometers (should be the type
     on a metal or plastic backing suitable for mounting)

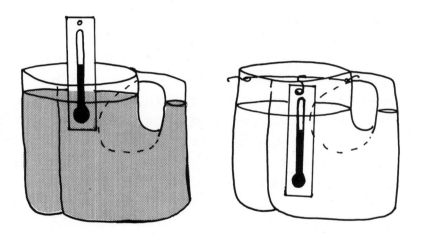

Cut the tops off both jugs. Use the scissors to poke a small hole near the top of two opposite sides of one jug. Fill this jug with water and the other one with dirt. Thread a string through the two holes, forming a line across the water. Compare the two thermometers and record the temperature readings if they aren't the same. Bend the paper clip into a hook and use it to suspend one thermometer in the water. Bury the bulb end of the other thermometer in the dirt. Place the two containers side by side outdoors in a sunny spot. Be sure they are shielded from the wind. Check the temperature readings after thirty minutes and again after an hour. Which shows the greatest increase?

3. You'll need:
   a piece of aluminum foil
   dirt
   two shoe boxes
   two indoor/outdoor
     thermometers

Cover the bottom of one box with aluminum foil—shiny side up. Cover the bottom of the other box with dirt. Place the two boxes side by side outdoors in a sunny spot. Be sure they are shielded from the wind. Compare the two thermometers and record the temperature readings if they aren't the same. Lay one thermometer on the bottom of each box. Wait thirty minutes and check the temperature readings. Which shows the greatest increase?

Based on what you've discovered, decide which of these places absorb most of the infrared rays that strike them and which reflect most of the energy away: a lake, a polar ice cap, an asphalt parking lot, a sandy beach, dark rocks, a field of corn, and a light-colored cement driveway.

The infrared rays that reach the earth from the sun are called short-wave radiation. Things that absorb this radiation are warmed and in turn give off heat energy in the form of long-wave radiation. While short-wave radiation can easily pass through clouds, long-wave radiation can't. So the heat waves radiated from the earth are trapped and bounced back. This is called the *greenhouse effect* because

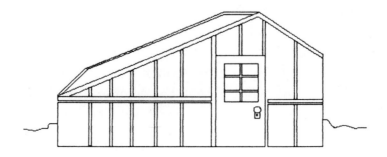

glass also traps long-wave radiation, making the air inside a green-house much warmer than the air outside. Try this investigation to see how this heat trap works.

Line the insides of two boxes with black paper (or paint them black) and lay an indoor/outdoor thermometer on the bottom of each. Put the boxes side by side outdoors in a sunny spot. Be sure they're shielded from the wind. Compare the two thermometers and record the temperature readings if they aren't exactly the same. Then cover one box with a piece of glass or clear wrap. Check the temperatures again after thirty minutes. The covered box will show the greater temperature increase. If you've ever gotten into a closed-up car that has been sitting in full sun, you've felt the greenhouse effect. Leave a thermometer inside a closed car on a sunny day to see just how much hotter it is inside than out. Can you see why it is particularly dangerous to leave pets and small children in a closed car even for a few minutes during the summer?

PUZZLER ANSWER

Heat lightning is lightning. (See page 131 for more information about what causes lightning.) It's just too far away for you to see the bolts or hear the thunder. What you see is a bright flash lighting up the sky and clouds for an instant.

Seeing Heat

YOU CAN'T see heat, but rattlesnakes and other snakes called pit vipers can. These animals have a special infrared-sensitive organ located beneath each eye. By turning their heads until the signals received from each heat-sensitive pit are balanced, they can locate and catch prey, such as mice, in total darkness. You aren't able to see that something is warm until it reaches about 1,292°F (700°C) and glows red-hot.

PUZZLER

The daytime temperature in the Sahara Desert in northern Africa might be 126°F (52.2°C), but the nighttime temperature only 26°F (−3.3°C). How could any place so hot during the day be so cold at night?

(See page 51.)

Measured in The Shade

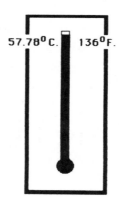

57.78°C.   136°F.

THE THERMOMETER pictured above shows the highest temperature ever recorded in the shade. That record was set at Al'Aziziyah (also spelled El Azizia), Libya, on September 13, 1922. There isn't any information about how hot it was in full sun on that historic day. However, you can find out how much hotter it is in the sun than in the shade where you live. You'll need an indoor/outdoor thermometer.

Place the thermometer outdoors in a sunny place that is shielded from the wind. Wait thirty minutes before checking the temperature reading, and write down the results. Repeat this test in a shady spot. How much cooler is it in the shade? Compare the same sunny and shady locations early in the morning, at noon, and late in the afternoon. Is there a greater temperature difference at one time of day than another? Why do you think it's important to make all these tests in exactly the same location? Are some shady spots cooler than others? How could you set up an investigation to find out?

Shade with Shape

THAT'S WHAT a shadow is. On a sunny morning, set a hardcover book upright on white cement, spreading the cover enough that it will stand alone. Then outline the book's shadow with a piece of chalk. Light travels in a straight line, and the book's shadow is the area the sunlight can't reach. The shadow is slanting away in the direction opposite to where the sunlight is coming from. The brighter the day, the more contrast there will be between the lit and the blocked area. So shadows are more distinct on a sunny day than on a somewhat cloudy day.

You already know from making your own sundial that as the sun appears to travel (it's actually the earth that is rotating) in an arc across the sky, an object's shadow moves, too. How big the shadow is depends on the way the light rays strike the object. A shadow ends where the first light rays clear the top of the object. Light rays are slanted early in the morning and again late in the afternoon because the sun is low in the sky. At those times, shadows stretch long and skinny. At noon, because the sun is almost directly overhead, light rays are nearly vertical. Then shadows are short and fat. Many ancient people believed that their shadows were separate, special parts of themselves that needed to be protected. According to one African legend, people who went outside at noon were in danger of having their shadows disappear forever.

Leave the book on the cement and check its shadow every hour or two. Use different colors of chalk to outline the book's shadow again at noon and at two o'clock. Notice how the length of the shadow as well as its direction changes in response to the sun's position in the sky.

Shadow Hunt

GO ON a shadow hunt in the morning or late in the afternoon, when shadows are the most dramatic. Take along a metal measuring tape (the kind contractors use), a pencil, and a pad of paper. When you find one of the shadows in the list below, place a piece of paper so the shadow falls on it. Then trace the shadow. If the shadow is too big or there isn't room to place your paper so the shadow will fall on it, draw what the shadow looks like. Try to be as careful as you can about copying the slant and general shape. Be sure to write down what object's shadow you've captured. Also write down the shadow's length and width.

When you go hunting, see if you can find:
1. The littlest shadow
2. The biggest shadow
3. The skinniest shadow
4. The roundest shadow

5. The oddest-looking shadow
6. A shadow with at least one hole in it (a hole in a shadow will appear as a bright spot).

If you have a camera available—particularly one that develops pictures automatically—take snapshots of your friends' shadows. Be sure to capture the whole person, and for the most fun make these photos of shadows in action. Number the pictures and make a corresponding list of names so you can identify each person's shadow. Then, the next time your friends get together, pass around the prints. Challenge them to find their own shadows. Can they identify one another's shadows?

Shadow Tag

THIS is a fun game for a sunny day. You'll need to play on light-colored cement so the shadows will show. This game is played like regular tag except that the person who is "it" tries to step on the other players' shadows rather than tap them. When do you think this game would be more difficult for the person who is "it"—at noon or at three o'clock in the afternoon?

Measuring Shadows

YOU CAN USE shadows to find out how tall some big things really are. You'll need a meter stick, a metal measuring tape (the kind contractors use), and a friend's help. Maybe you've wondered just how tall the giant flagpole at a local car dealership is. At noon on a sunny day, hold a meter stick close to the pole's shadow with one end touching the ground. Keep your own shadow out of the way while your friend measures the meter stick's shadow. Write down how long it is. Then figure out how much longer than a meter this is. If the shadow is two meters, it's twice as long. Next, measure the flagpole's shadow. The ratio of the length of the pole's shadow to the pole's height will be the same as the ratio between the meter stick's shadow and its length. If the meter stick's shadow was twice as long as the actual stick, divide the length of the flagpole's shadow by two to discover how tall the pole really is.

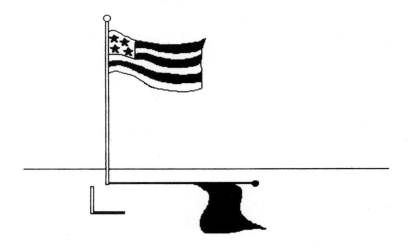

WEATHER TRIVIA

The eastern Sahara Desert in northern Africa has more than 4,300 hours of sunlight every year.

PUZZLER ANSWER

It's common for there to be a big difference between daytime and nighttime temperatures in the desert because there isn't enough moisture to produce clouds. Without clouds to trap the heat, the bare earth quickly radiates away the heat energy that has built up during the day.

Fake Shadows

DOES a tall giraffe have trouble finding a place to hide? No, the large, liver-shaped spots on its coat are like shadows. As the giraffe wanders, nibbling, among the acacia trees on the African veld (plain), its whole body blends in. A fawn's spotted coat is also a trick. This makes the fawn look like sunlit patches among dry leaves. Before World War I, soldiers wore brightly colored uniforms. Then leaders realized that it was smarter to be less noticeable. Ever since, combat uniforms and even such equipment as jeeps and tanks have been painted in a mottled design resembling a leafy pattern of bright spots and shadows.

Can a Shadow Smile?

BEFORE cameras, people often had their silhouettes done. A tracing was made of the shadow of a person's profile. Can you guess why the profile and not the full-face shadow was used? This outline was usually cut out of dark paper and mounted on a light background. You can do this kind of portrait, too. Work inside in a darkened room so you can control the sharpness of the shadow. You'll need a bright light, such as a slide projector or a lamp without its shade.

Have the person whose portrait you're doing stand or sit sideways so that the light makes his or her shadow profile fall on a wall or door. You may change the position of the light or have the person move closer to the wall or door to make the shadow sharp and distinct. Can the shadow adequately capture a smiling expression, or does the silhouette look better when the person isn't smiling? Experiment until the image is just what you want.

Then tape a piece of white paper on the wall or door (check first to be sure where you're allowed to do this) so the shadow profile falls on it. Outline the shadow with a pencil. Most silhouettes include the neck and shoulders. Next, cut out the outline and use this as a pattern to transfer the image to dark paper. Cut out the silhouette and mount it on light-colored paper. For a special effect, you may want to alternate some light and dark details on the clothing as shown in the example.

Built-in Shade and Some You Can Pour On

PEOPLE NEED some exposure to sunlight because the sun's rays trigger the production of vitamin D by the skin. Without adequate amounts of this vitamin, the body wouldn't be able to use calcium from milk and other foods to build strong teeth and bones. However, too much exposure to the sun's ultraviolet rays can burn the skin and damage delicate tissues. You may be exposed to even more than you realize if you're on a sandy beach by the water— both areas reflect the sun's radiation. Burning ultraviolet rays slip through even on cloudy days when you don't feel hot.

When you go outside during the summer, it's best to leave your skin unprotected for only ten to fifteen minutes at first. You can gradually increase your exposure time as your skin builds up its natural protection. Just as *Star Trek's* spaceship *Enterprise* activates a force field, your skin creates a sun shield by increasing production of special pigment granules called melanin. These granules are what give your skin its natural color. A temporary increase in the melanin level is a tan. Of course, you can still burn even if you have a tan or naturally dark skin, if you're exposed to the sun's ultraviolet rays for too long at one time. Suntan lotions containing the additive PABA (para-aminobenzoic acid) can help protect you from sunburn. The compound called PABA absorbs the burning ultraviolet radiation before it can reach your skin.

If you do get a sunburn, treat it like any other burn. Cool, wet cloths will make your skin feel better, particularly if the area swells. If blisters form, be careful not to break them. An infection could start. If large areas are badly sunburned, you may feel nauseous and have a headache. You'll need a doctor's help for a bad sunburn.

Too Much Heat

MOST ANIMALS can survive only in a narrow temperature range. Cold-blooded animals, such as frogs, fish, and snakes, have their body temperatures regulated by their environment. They usually can't live if temperatures go above 90°F (33.89°C) for very long. If it gets too hot, some animals estivate. Just like an animal that hibernates through the winter, animals that estivate have their heart and breathing rates greatly reduced. The antelope ground squirrel, which lives in the desert regions of the southwestern United States, for example, sleeps away the hottest part of the summer, living off the food stored within its body.

A person exposed to too much heat can suffer from heat exhaustion or heat stroke. In either case, he or she won't feel well. If you suspect this is the problem, feel the person's skin. Cool and sweaty means heat exhaustion. Have that person drink a half-glass of water with two pinches of salt mixed in and then lie down to rest. Periodically, provide another half-glass of water with salt until the skin no longer feels cool and sweaty.

If the skin feels hot and dry, the person is suffering from heat stroke. This is more serious because it means the body is no longer handling the heat. Immediately move the person to the shade and pour on plenty of water to lower the body temperature. That person will need to see a doctor as soon as possible.,

Hot Fish

A FISH called *Barbus thermalis* not only doesn't mind the heat, it thrives on being hot. This fish lives in hot springs in Sri Lanka, where the water temperatures average 122°F (50°C).

Making a Solar Still

YOU CAN USE the sun's heat energy to provide a drink of fresh water even in the middle of the desert.

You'll need:

> a shovel
> a sheet of medium-to-heavy-gauge plastic about
>   18 inches (45.7 centimeters) square—a large
>   clean garbage bag cut open will do
> a glass
> several rocks
> a small stone

First, dig a hole about 12 inches (30.5 centimeters) deep and 12 inches (30.5 centimeters) square. If possible, pat the sides smooth so they won't crumble. Next, place the glass in the bottom and cover the hole with the plastic. Use the stone to make the plastic sag over the glass. Anchor the edges of the plastic sheet with the rocks. There shouldn't be an opening for air to slip in.

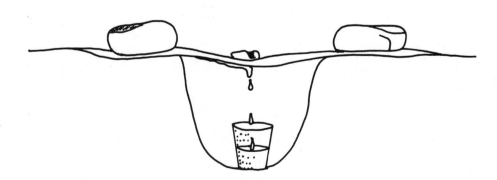

As the heat builds up inside the hole, moisture from the ground will evaporate (change from a liquid to a gas). Eventually, as the air inside the hole becomes saturated with the moisture, droplets will form on the plastic, roll down the sloping sheet, and drip into the glass. A special kind of solar still is supplied as part of the survival gear for pilots who might have to ditch at sea. Saltwater is poured into a plastic bag, which is then inflated. As the temperature rises, the seawater evaporates, leaving the salt behind. The water droplets that form are fresh water. This is funneled into a separate holding tank. Such a solar still can usually produce about 1 quart (1 liter) of fresh water a day.

Cooking With Sunshine

I F YOU CAN concentrate the rays, you can even use the sun's heat energy for cooking. Follow these directions to make your own solar hot dog cooker.

You'll need:

- a round container, such as oatmeal comes in
- tape
- scissors
- aluminum foil
- a wire coat hanger
- wire cutters
- a hot dog

1. Cut a large opening in the side of the container as shown. Tape the lid on tight.

2. Line the inside with foil—shiny side out.

3. Use the wire cutters to cut the coat hanger. You may want an adult's help with this. Bend the metal into a rod with a hook on the end.

4. With the pointed end of the scissors, poke a hole big enough for the metal rod to go through

in either end of the
container.

5. Stick the rod through
   one hole. Then push it
   through the length of
   the hot dog and out the
   other end of the
   container.

6. Hold your solar cooker
   so the opening is aimed
   at the sun. Periodically,
   turn your hot dog.

7. To speed up cooking,
   you may want to try
   propping up a mirror so
   it also focuses sunlight
   on the hot dog.

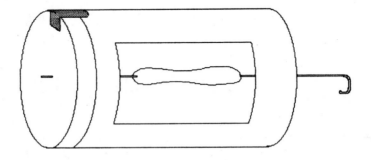

How long does it take the hot dog to get done?

Sun Tea

NO NEED to put a tea kettle on
to boil to produce iced tea. Fill a
gallon jug with water. Put in two
tea bags, cover tightly, and set
the container outside in the sunshine. When the brew looks as
dark as you like it, pour some
over ice. How nice!

Hard-Boiled Eggs

IN HOT AREAS, birds that nest on the ground can't leave their eggs uncovered. They'll cook. Only the largest egg, the ostrich's egg, which weighs as much as 4 pounds (1.8 kilograms), can survive prolonged exposure to the sun.

Sunlight Wins the War

ONCE, LONG AGO, a Greek port city was surprised by the attack of a fleet of Roman warships. The soldiers of the town gathered, ready to defend the community, but it was obvious that they would be outnumbered. The Greek city seemed doomed.

Archimedes, a Greek noted for his scientific investigations, lived there. Watching the town prepare to face the enemy, he had an idea. Quickly he convinced a group of soldiers to go with him to the cliff above the harbor. He had the men stand close together, holding their highly polished shields in front of them. On his signal, the soldiers tipped their shields at just the right angle to catch the sunlight and reflect the rays to the Roman ships. The wooden hulls burst into flame. The ships sank in the harbor, and the city was saved.

This is only a legend. It's unlikely that anyone could have focused the sun's rays on a bobbing ship long enough to generate the heat needed to ignite the wood. However, there are experimental solar furnaces in operation today capable of concentrating the sun's energy and producing tremendous heat. One, on Mont Louis in the French Pyrenees Mountains, has a bank of mirrors that are controlled by a computer to track the sun. The captured rays are bounced to a parabolic (bowl-shaped) reflector made up of over 9,500 tiny mirrors. A focused beam from this reflector can generate temperatures of about 6,300°F (3,500°C).

Send Sun Messages

BECAUSE light can be reflected from anything shiny, you can use the sun to send signals. In fact, the heliograph, a device used to flash the sun's rays, is a very old tool for transmitting messages. One of the most extensive and long-range uses of the heliograph was made in the 1870s by General Nelson A. Miles. He established stations on mountain peaks in New Mexico and Arizona, creating a network to keep track of warring Apache Indians. Through this network, signals were often flashed as far as 50 miles (80.5 kilometers).

Sunlight travels in a straight path and will be blocked by any obstacle. So don't expect your message to go around a corner or through a building. A small hand mirror makes a good heliograph. Traditionally, Morse code has been used. Dots are represented by short flashes. Dashes are shown as long flashes. However, you could make up a shortcut code of your own, such as:

two long flashes	"Yes"
two short flashes	"No"
two long flashes and a short	"Can you play?"
two short flashes and a long	"Meet you at the corner."

Sun Day Your Prints Will Come

YOU'LL NEED: studio proof paper and a 6-ounce (168-gram) package of fixer (both can be purchased where photographic supplies are sold) a piece of poster board, tape, a plastic bucket, a quart jar, water, paper towels, a watch with a second hand, and ice tongs.

Fold the poster board in half, forming an envelope, and tape three sides shut. Use this to carry a piece of the proof paper out into the sun so you won't risk exposing the rest of the package.

Plan in advance what objects you'll print. Things with interesting shapes are best. Pour 1 quart (1 liter) of lukewarm water into the bucket, dump in the fixer, and stir with the tongs. When the powder is completely dissolved, carry your equipment outside. Place a sheet of proof paper flat in a sunny spot—shiny side up—and arrange the objects on it. Then let it sit for two minutes.

Pick up the exposed paper with the tongs and ease it into the fixer. After two minutes, wiggle the paper with the tongs to slosh the solution over it and wait an additional two minutes. The timing doesn't have to be exact—just close. Lift your sun print out of the fixer and lay it on a paper towel to dry. Proof paper is treated with a chemical that changes in sunlight. The paper will darken everywhere it wasn't shielded from the sun's rays by an object. What you've created is a sort of shadow in reverse.

Spreading Sunlight

ON A HOT, sunny day, turn on the hose and spray water into the air. Slowly shift your position until the light shining through the droplets creates a rainbow, shimmering in the mist. Sunlight is actually a bundle of different kinds of light. These all travel at the same speed—the speed of light, or 186,000 miles (300,000 kilometers) per second—but each has its own amount of energy and its own wavelength. Light waves have valleys and crests just like swells on the ocean. The wavelength is the distance between two crests.

When sunlight passes through the water droplets, each kind of light wave is refracted (bent) a slightly different amount from the others. So the bundle spreads, allowing you to see the individual colors.

What color do you see at the top of the rainbow? What color is at the bottom? Have someone else hold the hose while you use crayons to color a copy of the spectrum (series of color bands arranged in order of their respective wavelengths) on a piece of paper.

Are you getting pretty warm exploring summer? Are you feeling tempted to spray some water over your head? It's not a bad way to cool off. The next chapter is full of ways to beat the heat. Read on.

3.
KEEPING COOL

The Duel

THE SUN and the North Wind had been arguing all morning about who was strongest. "Ho, I'll prove my powers are greater than yours, Sun," shouted North Wind. "See that man?" Below them, a lone traveler was trudging along a dusty road. He was wearing a cap and a jacket. "Whichever of us can make him take off that hat will be the champion."

When the Sun accepted the challenge, the North Wind nearly laughed. He had tricked the Sun. One quick puff and he'd blow off the man's cap. The North Wind puffed up bigger and bigger. Then all at once he blew. The harsh, cold wind swirled around the man, and he put one hand on his cap. Angered, the North Wind blew even harder. The man leaned into the wind and clutched the cap, holding it on his head. Exhausted at last, the North Wind hissed, "It's hopeless."

The Sun didn't comment but began to glow more and more warmly. The man soon took off his jacket and folded it over one arm. The Sun continued to beam. Smiling, the man took off his cap.

According to this legend, the Sun won the duel, proving that gentle persuasion is sometimes more powerful than brute force. The story also shows, however, that when the weather gets hot, people do what they can to cool off.

Climate Control

WHEN the temperature rises, your body automatically starts trying to cool itself. First, your natural circulation changes. More blood is pumped through the capillaries, tiny blood vessels just beneath your skin. This allows your internal heat energy to reach the surface and be radiated away. Then, the nearly two million sweat glands in your skin activate, pouring a liquid called perspiration or sweat out through your pores.

Look at your skin with a magnifying glass to see the many tiny openings—pores. How much liquid flows out onto your skin will vary depending on how warm the weather is and how much heat you're generating by being active. As the sweat evaporates, some of your heat energy is used to speed up the molecules changing the liquid sweat to a gas, and you feel cooler. Sweating is so important to keeping the body from overheating that in Egypt people sometimes greet each other with the expression "How do you sweat?"

To experience this cooling effect "first hand," put on a pair of cotton gardening gloves—or pull cotton tube socks on like mittens. Dip one gloved hand into a bucket of water and then sit in the sunshine. After five minutes, which hand feels cooler—the wet one or the dry one? If you're willing to sit there long enough, you'll see that

when the cloth eventually dries, the cooling effect is lost. Watch out! By that time, you might be overheated and sunburned.

Wind helps your body's natural cooling efforts. Wet both gloved hands. Then let one hang down at your side while you wave the other one above your head. Which hand feels cooler this time? The hand you're waving will, because moving air speeds up evaporation. Wind also carries away radiated heat more quickly. Can you explain now why it was important to shield the thermometers from the wind when you performed the investigations in "Bouncing Heat"?

You can't always count on evaporation to cool you off, however. Air can hold only so much moisture. The amount of moisture in the air compared to what it can hold is the relative humidity. It's presented as a percentage, with 100 percent showing complete saturation. A hygrometer is an instrument that measures the relative humidity, and you can make one to check how much moisture is in the air. You'll need two indoor/outdoor thermometers and a wet paper towel.

Place the thermometers outdoors side by side where they will be shielded from the wind. Wrap the wet paper towel over the bulb end of one of the thermometers. Check both temperature readings after thirty minutes. Subtract the wet bulb reading from the dry bulb reading and use the chart to find the relative humidity.

Dry Bulb Temperature in °C/°F

	5/41	6/43	7/45	8/46	9/48	10/50	11/52	12/54	13/55	14/57	15/59	16/61	17/62	18/64	19/66	20/68	21/70	22/72	23/73	24/75
1	86	86	87	87	88	88	89	89	90	90	90	90	90	91	91	91	92	92	92	92
2	72	73	74	75	76	77	78	78	79	79	80	81	81	82	82	83	83	83	84	84
3	58	60	62	63	64	66	67	68	69	70	71	71	72	73	74	74	75	76	76	77
4	45	48	50	51	53	55	56	58	59	60	61	63	64	65	65	66	67	68	69	69
5	33	35	38	40	42	44	46	48	50	51	53	54	55	57	58	59	60	61	62	62
6	20	24	26	29	32	34	36	39	41	42	44	46	47	49	50	51	53	54	55	56
7	7	11	15	19	22	24	27	29	32	34	36	38	40	41	43	44	46	47	48	49
8				8	12	15	18	21	23	26	27	30	32	34	36	37	39	40	42	43
9						6	9	12	15	18	20	23	25	27	29	31	32	34	36	37
10									7	10	13	15	18	20	22	24	26	28	30	31
11											6	8	11	14	16	18	20	22	24	26
12														7	10	12	14	17	19	20

Difference Between Dry-Bulb and Wet-Bulb Temperature

Warm air can hold more moisture than cool air because the molecules are farther apart. When the humidity is high, sweat won't evaporate. Then the moisture on your skin makes you feel even hotter. Where it's very dry, such as in certain hot desert areas, people can endure temperatures up to 200°F (93.33°C) for as long as several hours at a time. If there is 100 percent humidity, however, people may suffer from heat exhaustion or heat stroke when the temperature goes over 90°F (32.22°C).

The Unsweet Smell of Summer

IF SOMETHING stinks, it could be you. Sweat glands help filter wastes out of your blood. So sweat contains mineral salts—that's why you taste salty if you've ever licked your sweaty arm—and urea, the same waste product that's in urine. When the liquid evaporates, the minerals and wastes are left behind, building up on your skin. This may act as a natural insect repellent, but it can keep your friends at a distance, too.

PUZZLER

> *On a hot, humid day, would you feel cooler if you ate a tossed salad or tacos with jalapeño peppers?*
>
> *(See page 73.)*

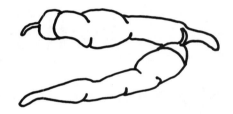

Start a Fan Club

IF THERE aren't any natural breezes blowing, you can create your own. Fold a piece of plain white paper accordion-style, as shown below. For a more interesting windmaker, draw and color a design on the paper before folding. Then gather the pleats together at one side. Wrap tape around the bunched folds to form a handle.

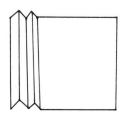

Or color a design on the front of two paper plates. Tape a paint stick to the back of one plate. Then spread white glue on the back of the other plate and press this over the stick and the first plate.

The ancient Assyrians and Egyptians often used large leaves for fans. Raffia palms (from Madagascar and the islands of Japan) and Amazonian bamboo palms (from South America) have leaves up to 65 feet (19.8 meters) long. Can you find a big leaf that you could use as a fan? The folding fan is believed to have originated in Japan about 700 A.D. During the 1800s, fans became works of art. Some were hand-painted with fanciful designs. Others were made of ostrich or peacock feathers. Men as well as women carried fans. The Japanese even had a war fan made of iron and leather. With that fan, a soldier could both keep cool and defend himself.

Wetter Is Better

YOU CAN HELP your body's natural cooling system and have fun doing it. How about squirt guns at twenty paces? Or maybe a water-balloon toss?

For this, each person will need to fill a balloon with water, knotting the neck to seal it. Then draw two lines 2 yards (1.8 meters) apart on a sidewalk or driveway—or place two pieces of rope on a grassy yard—for opponents to face each other. On a starting signal, players begin tossing and catching the water balloons. To make the event more challenging, have players take one step back from the line after each throw. The winner is the last player holding an unbroken balloon. On a really hot day, though, it can be more fun to lose.

For a thrill, try the bucket chiller. Fill a plastic bucket with a handle, such as ice cream sometimes comes in, with water. Hold the bucket handle in one hand and stand outside in an open area. Check to be sure you won't hit anything or anyone. Then, keeping your arm straight, swing the bucket in a big circle—upside down and around. If you swing the bucket fast enough, the water will stay in the bucket even when it's upside down. Stopping is the hard part. Try both a gradual slowdown and a sudden halt. Which lets more water slosh out of the bucket?

Swimming is a fun way to stay wet, but only if done safely. Join a Red Cross swimming program in your community to learn strokes and water safety. Then remember:

Never swim alone.
Always swim only where you know it's safe—safe areas will
have a lifeguard and be clearly marked.

Here is a list of some of the ways you can swim, and world records for those strokes.

Stroke	Distance	Time Minutes:Seconds	Champion
FREESTYLE Men	100 meters	49.36	Ambrose (Rowdy) Gaines (U.S.), 1981
Women		54.79	Barbara Krause (E. Germany), 1980
BREASTSTROKE Men	100 meters	1:02.13	John Moffet (U.S.), 1984
Women		1:08.51	Ute Geweniger (E. Germany), 1983
BUTTERFLY Men	100 meters	53.38	Pablo Morales (U.S.), 1984
Women		57.93	Mary Meagher (U.S.), 1981
BACKSTROKE Men	100 meters	55.19	Richard (Rick) Carey (U.S.), 1983
Women		1:00.86	Rica Reinisch (E. Germany), 1980

Unless you have had life-saving training, don't try to swim to rescue someone who might be drowning. Instead, use something to reach out to that person, such as a pole, a towel, or a rope. If the distance is too great, throw the victim something that will float and go for help.

Super Splash

THE WORLD'S largest swimming pool is the Orthlieb Pool in Casa-blanca, Morocco. This saltwater pool is a mini-ocean covering 8.9 acres (3.6 hectares). At the Wet N' Wild water-action amusement park, you can climb the world's highest slide for a long glide into the water. Called Der Stuka, this ride is 75 feet (22.9 meters) high and 400 feet (122 meters) long. In the wave pool, you can ride on swells that rise more than 3 feet (.9 meters) in the deep end.

Fish Race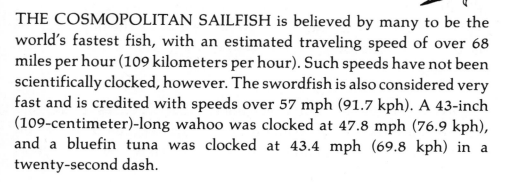

THE COSMOPOLITAN SAILFISH is believed by many to be the world's fastest fish, with an estimated traveling speed of over 68 miles per hour (109 kilometers per hour). Such speeds have not been scientifically clocked, however. The swordfish is also considered very fast and is credited with speeds over 57 mph (91.7 kph). A 43-inch (109-centimeter)-long wahoo was clocked at 47.8 mph (76.9 kph), and a bluefin tuna was clocked at 43.4 mph (69.8 kph) in a twenty-second dash.

PUZZLER ANSWER

You'd feel cooler if you ate the tossed salad. Spicy foods make you sweat, and if the weather is humid, the perspiration won't evaporate readily.

RIDDLE

Why did the chef put suntan lotion on the chicken?

He wanted to serve dark meat.

Moist on the Inside

YOUR BODY is 60 percent water. When you sweat, your body loses some of its essential fluids. Just how much you sweat varies, and so does the amount of replacement liquid you need. However, you'll need about 1 quart (1 liter) a day—at least. Here are some tasty alternatives to pouring yourself a glass of water.

Fruit Whip: You'll need one 16-ounce can of crushed pineapple or mandarin oranges, one 16-ounce can of fruit cocktail, and one banana (sliced). Combine these ingredients in a blender and puree. Pour into paper cups and freeze until solid. To eat, tear away the upper part of the cup—leave the lower part for easy holding. Rip away more paper as needed.

Ice Pack: Freeze the individual-serving sized drink boxes (preferably those that are 100 percent fruit juice) until they're solid. Then, when you're off to explore, put one in a pocket. You'll have a portable cooling system and a slush to sip when it's thawed.

Orange Cow: You'll need a tall glass, two scoops of vanilla ice cream, orange juice, a spoon and a straw. Put the ice cream into the glass and fill with orange juice. Drink up!

A Drink in Every Bite

WATERMELONS are 93 percent water. That's a lot of juice considering that while most watermelons weigh from 5 to 40 pounds (2.3 to 18 kilograms), some can weigh as much as 100 pounds (45 kilograms). If you want to grow some, you'll need plenty of room. These melons grow on long trailing stems called runners that can stretch for 40 feet (12.2 meters). Tendrils grow out of the vines to anchor the plants and keep the big melons from rolling in a high wind. While a lot of watermelons are eaten in the United States, Turkey and China grow the most. Two new varieties, Triple Sweet and Tri X 313, are seedless, but don't get one of those. Part of the fun of eating a watermelon is spitting out the seeds. Just be sure you're outside when you try these events:

1. *Distance spit.* It will be easier to spot the shiny black seeds on light-colored cement. Use chalk to mark a spitting line. Next, measure and mark off lines 6 feet (1.8 meters), 12 feet (3.7 meters), and so forth from this point. Then pass out the melon slices and challenge your friends to see who can spit the farthest.

2. *Sure shot.* Can you hit a plastic bucket from 6 feet (1.8 meters)? Can you hit a smaller target, such as soup can, from that distance?

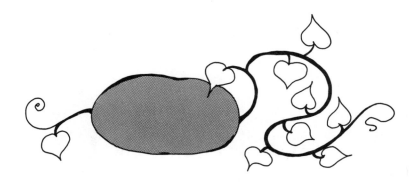

Digging Up a Drink

ON AN AVERAGE HOT DAY, an elephant drinks 50 gallons (189.3 liters) of water. So what does an elephant do when it can't find any water? It digs a well. First the elephant selects the site—usually the bottom of a dried-up riverbed. Then it uses its tusks like shovels to dig into the hard ground. The elephant may also stomp on the ground with its big feet. When wet soil is reached, the elephant uses its trunk to scoop out dirt until the hole fills with water. After the elephant moves on, other thirsty animals gather for a sip.

The Sweet Chill

THE ICE CREAM SODA was invented in 1874. The ice cream cone was developed at the World's Fair in St. Louis in 1904—a way to serve and eat ice cream without a bowl and a spoon. The Eskimo Pie was created in 1921 and was followed seven years later by ice cream on a stick. The United States leads the world in ice cream production and eating. On the average, each and every person in the United States consumes 15 quarts (14.2 liters) a year. Australians, New Zealanders, and Swedes are close behind as ice cream fans.

Cool Dressing

THE SECRET to staying cool and comfortable is to allow the most air possible to circulate past your skin while protecting yourself from the sun's burning rays. How much you cover up will depend partly on the intensity of the sunshine where you live. In general, to be cool and sun-safe, you should wear:

A straw hat (large weave that allows air circulation) to shade your face

Sunglasses—photogray is considered the most effective sunscreen color

Suntan lotion with the highest available PABA content

Neck scarf or headband (optional) to help absorb perspiration

A 100 percent cotton shirt

Underwear that isn't too tight

Shorts with open legs and a loose-fitting waistband

Sandals or cotton tube socks and canvas tennis shoes

How Animals Beat the Heat

ANIMALS that live where it's hot have some special adaptations for keeping cool.

Elephants

WHEN these land giants get too hot, they flap their big ears. Blood circulating through the network of blood vessels close to the surface of the skin radiates away excess body heat. African elephants, which live south of the Sahara Desert, have even larger ears than Asiatic elephants, which inhabit India and Southeast Asia. If ear flapping isn't enough to cool it down, an elephant snuffs up a trunkful of cool water and sprays it over its

back. An adult elephant trunk can hold 6 liters (1.5 gallons) at a sniff. Or the elephant may go for a swim, holding its trunk out of the water like a snorkel. Elephants can't rub on suntan lotion to protect their sensitive skin, but they do roll in the mud. When the mud dries, the elephants have an effective sun shield.

DUST LIGHTLY

The bushmen of the Kalahari Desert in Africa also use dirt to protect their skin. They smear themselves with oil. Then the oil collects dust, forming a thick coating that is an effective sunscreen.

Kangaroo Rats

THESE DESERT rodents don't sweat, but if their body temperature nears the lethal level of ·107.6°F (42°C), they salivate heavily. This drool wets the animals' chins and throats, cooling them off just enough. Usually kangaroo rats simply escape the heat by slipping into their burrows. Once underground they plug the opening with dirt. More than shutting out the heat

and enemies, this closed-door policy holds in the moisture they breathe out. The kangaroo rat is one of the few animals that never drinks water. The water needed for bodily functions is produced through the digestive process. In the desert, holding onto water is just as important as staying cool.

Antelope Ground Squirrels

AT HOME in the deserts of the southwestern United States, these animals are experts at cooling off. When their body temperature starts to shoot up, they pant. If they're still too hot, they'll dive into a burrow or flatten their bodies against the ground in a shady spot. Spreading out helps the antelope ground squirrel conduct body heat away through direct contact with the cooler ground, in addition to radiating excess heat away into the air. Within three minutes these animals can drop their body temperature from 107.6°F (42°C) to 91.4°F (33°C)—an important difference. In an emergency they will also drool heavily to wet their paws and head for the cooling effect of evaporation. Despite their ability to stay cool, antelope ground squirrels usually simply escape the heat of a hot desert summer by estivating.

Desert Tortoises

THE THICK SHELL on its back is like having a built-in umbrella for shade. However, even with this portable protection, the desert tortoise usually stays in its burrow during the hottest part of the day. It can stand body temperatures of about 105°F (40.6°C), but if it gets hotter, it also salivates so evaporation will cool it down. Desert tortoises not only know how to beat the heat, they use it. They mate and lay their eggs in June. Then, while the sun's heat incubates their eggs, the parents estivate, sleeping away the hottest weeks of the summer.

Ships of the Desert

CAMELS got this nickname because of their rocking gait and because they are especially suited to transporting people and cargo across hot, dry deserts. Camels can stand to have their body temperature increase as much as six degrees without any ill effects. If your temperature goes up even two degrees, you feel very sick. Camels have thick eyebrows to shade their eyes from the sun and thick, cushioned foot pads, which act like snowshoes to carry them over hot, shifting sands. While the camels' humps—Arabian camels (Dromedaries) have one; Bactrian camels have two—are full

of fat, a special process can convert this fat to water for bodily functions. Camels can go from two to five days without drinking, but they normally drink about 5 gallons (19 liters) of water a day. They are herbivores, grazing on whatever plants are available. The linings of their mouths are so tough, camels can even eat cactus—spines and all.

In 1857 the U.S. Army imported eighty camels from Africa and Asia with the idea of using them as pack animals in the dry, hot desert of the southwestern United States. The U.S. Camel Corps' first job was to map a safe wagon route through the wilderness area between Fort Defiance, New Mexico, and the Colorado River. Edward Fitzgerald Beale successfully led the experimental caravan. Then the Camel Corps went on to California, setting up a second post. The camels carried mail and supplies back and forth across the desert for several years.

The Army planned to buy one thousand more camels and expand the duties performed by the Corps. The Civil War broke out, however, and the operation was put on hold. By the end of the war, the railroads had taken over the job of transporting mail and cargo. The camels were auctioned off to circuses and zoos. Those that weren't sold were set free. Wild camels continued to be spotted in the Sonoran Desert until 1941.

Are there any descendants of the original Camel Corps camels left? It's hard to say. You can follow in the first camel caravan's tracks, however. The wagon route Beale mapped became U.S. Highway 66 across Arizona.

PUZZLER

Why do wood shingles make a good roof for a house in a hot climate?

(See page 84.)

RIDDLE

What is kept in an air-conditioned vault?

Cold cash.

Heat Exchange

THERE IS a continual natural heat exchange. As air is heated, the molecules spread apart and the lighter air rises. Dense, cooler air sinks under the warmer air. You can prove this movement takes place. You'll need:

> an electric skillet, or a saucepan and a stove
> a glass pop bottle
> water
> a balloon

Stretch the neck of the balloon over the top of the bottle. Then pour enough water into the skillet or saucepan to cover the bottom. Set the bottle in the water and turn on the heat. Add water as necessary to be sure the pan doesn't go dry. As the air inside the bottle is heated, the balloon will fill and stretch up. The balloon is trapping the rising hot air. Then stand barefoot in front of a refrigerator and open the door. You'll feel cold air on your feet because this heavier air sinks as it rolls out.

This natural exchange means that if you live in a two-story house, the upstairs will be warmer than the downstairs. The coolest place in any room will be on the floor, and if your home has a basement, it will be the coolest spot in the house. Set up an investigation to find out just how much cooler it is downstairs than upstairs or on the floor than near the ceiling.

Since ancient times people have been trying to make their homes cooler when it's hot outside. In Egypt, where the desert air is dry as well as hot, people hung wet cloths across doors and windows. Evaporation cooled the air blowing in through these openings. The first modern air-cooling system was developed in the United States in 1920 by William H. Carrier, using refrigeration machinery.

An air conditioner has an inside and an outside unit. Inside, the warm room air is drawn past a coil filled with a refrigerant liquid. Heat energy is drawn from the air, causing the refrigerant to become a gas, and the now cool air is forced out into the room by a blower. Next, the compressor pumps the gas to the condenser in the outside unit. The condenser discharges heat from the refrigerant to the outside air, causing the gas to change back to a liquid. Finally, the refrigerant is returned to the coil in the inside unit to continue the cycle. Air-conditioning also helps you feel cooler by removing some of the humidity (moisture in the air) so perspiration will evaporate.

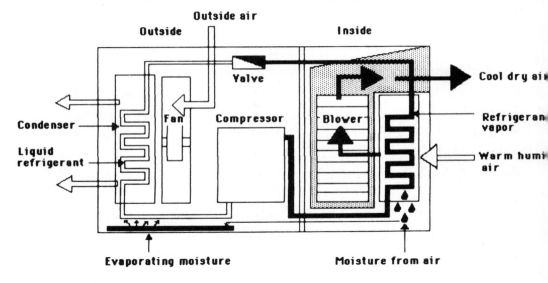

PUZZLER ANSWER

The wood shingles dry, shrink, and separate when it's hot, allowing heat rising from within the house to escape. When it rains, the wood shingles quickly swell, sealing the roof.

Don't get too comfortable inside. There's still a lot of exploring to do outside. You won't want to miss any of the adventures coming up in the next chapter.

4.
GOING
PLACES

Travels Into the Unknown

HAVE YOU ever dreamed of exploring a new frontier—of going where no one has ever been before? You can experience the flavor of venturing into the unknown even in the midst of some very familiar terrain. You'll need a compass, a pencil, a notebook, and a friend. It's always safer and more fun to share your adventure with someone. First, choose a starting point, such as the door to your apartment house or the mailbox on the corner, and write this in your notebook. Then list a set of directions that you'll follow, such as twenty paces north, ten paces east, thirty paces south, forty-five paces north, and twenty-five paces west. A pace is a double step—counted each time your right foot (or your left foot) comes down. Make your list of directions as long as you like. When it's complete, estimate how long your total journey should take, make a copy of your itinerary, and file this expedition plan with an adult—just in case a search party should be needed. Also be sure you have enough money to call and that you know someone you can reach if you should need help. Then go to your starting point.

Using the compass to determine your heading, follow the first instruction. Next, turn to face the new compass heading and proceed the number of paces indicated. As you travel, draw a map of your route, showing landmarks, such as a big dead tree or the name of a store. Unless you're in a wide-open area, don't be surprised when your directions lead you into an obstacle. Even famous explorers sometimes had to go around waterfalls, towering mountain peaks, and swamps. Mark the detour on your map. Then proceed on the next leg of your journey.

When you reach the end of your list, stop and look around. What is the place you've discovered like? Write down your observations. Is there any animal life? What type of plants, if any, do you see? Can you find a treasure—an unusual-looking rock, a bird feather, or something someone has dropped—to carry home with you? To find your way home, follow the map you drew or follow your list of directions in reverse.

If you have enough explorers, divide into teams for some group action. Each team creates a mystery route for the other to follow. First, everyone should agree on how many legs the journey will have. Ten is a good number. Each team will need a compass, a pencil, an index card for each segment of the trip, and a treasure. The team that establishes the route sets a starting point. Next, they list the compass heading and the number of paces to travel in that direction on the first index card. They will also include a message describing where to find the second clue when the first destination is reached. Then they will hide the second clue at that spot and go on. Each clue will send explorers to the next clue. The final clue will direct searchers to the treasure.

Once the routes are set up, the teams exchange starting clues and begin. For an added challenge, you may want to see which team can find their treasure in the least amount of time.

Snacks to Pack

Apple Cups: Wash an apple. Then cut it in half and remove the core. Mix together one-fourth cup of peanut butter, one-half teaspoon of honey, and two tablespoons of raisins. Fill the hollow of each apple half with this mixture. Tuck each half into a self-sealing plastic bag. This makes a treat for you and a friend.

Logs: Wash celery stalks and peel carrots. Cut both into short sticks. For an extra treat, fill the celery logs with peanut butter or cream cheese. Store these in self-sealing plastic bags.

How Far Have You Gone?

WONDER how far you've traveled? You'd know if you knew the average distance you go in one double step. You can figure this using a step course. On a sidewalk, a parking lot, or even an open field, mark a starting line. Then measure out 200 feet (60.9 meters) and put an ending marker.

Step out from the starting line with whichever foot you plan to count. Walk to the end marker and back to the starting line, keeping track of your double steps. Then divide the distance you covered— 400 feet (122 meters)—by the number of steps you took. The answer will tell you how many feet (meters) you covered with each step.

If you walk without stopping, how long you've traveled can also be a clue to how far you've walked. Across flat, open terrain, most people can walk 1 mile (1.6 kilometers) in fifteen minutes. In a wooded area, it usually takes about thirty minutes to walk the same distance.

PUZZLER

What are tumbleweeds?

(See page 92.)

RIDDLE

What is smaller than an insect's mouth?

Anything it eats.

Early Explorers in Hot Places

THE EARTH'S hot regions were settled by groups of people before there was a written history. Centuries later, explorers from other countries began to discover these areas. It's the story of their travels that has been recorded. However, these explorers were not always welcomed by the native residents. Sometimes they were even killed. Likewise, the explorers weren't always considerate of the rights of the native residents. Often the explorers became exploiters, claiming the land and its resources for their mother country.

Marcos de Niza (Spain) early 1500s	De Niza was a Franciscan priest in the service of Antonio de Mendoza, ruler of the Spanish colony in Mexico. He was sent to find the Seven Cities of Cibola, supposedly so rich that their walls were covered with gold and turquoise. He searched the desert of what is now the southwestern United States and finally found Hawiku'h, one of the seven cities. When he returned with an army a year later, however, and the city was conquered, the truth was revealed. The seven cities weren't rich at all.
Mungo Park (Scotland) 1795	Park led one of the first European expeditions to Africa. He was searching for the source and the mouth of the Niger River. He died during a second expedition to Africa. While he didn't find the source of the Niger, his efforts provided important information about the African interior.
Robert O'Hara Burke William Wills (England) 1860–1861	Much of Australia is desert. Burke and Wills made the first south to north crossing of Australia.
John McDouall Stuart (England) 1861–1862	Stuart made several expeditions into the interior of Australia, providing valuable information about the geology and plant life of this area. The route he chose was used in 1872 to lay a telegraph line that greatly aided exploration.

H. St. John Philby David Hogarth, T. E. Lawrence, and Bertram Thomas (England) World War I	*These men were among those who became familiar with much of northern Arabia while the British were fighting the Turkish army. T. E. Lawrence described this area and time in his book,* Seven Pillars of Wisdom. *Thomas's detailed notes showing compass headings, latitude readings, and altitudes made it possible to map a large part of the previously uncharted central portion of Arabia.*
Dr. Roy Chapman Andrews (United States) 1922	*The American Museum of Natural History sent Dr. Andrews to map the unexplored region of the Gobi Desert in eastern Asia and to find dinosaur fossils. His expedition was often short of water, and the men had to huddle in tents to escape fierce sandstorms. Dr. Andrews succeeded in mapping the previously uncharted Gobi and discovered fossils of many new types of dinosaurs. He even discovered the first fossil dinosaur eggs. You can see these at the American Museum of Natural History in New York City.*

PUZZLER ANSWER

Tumbleweeds are dried plants that are uprooted by the wind and blown across the desert. The Russian thistle is one of the most common tumbleweeds. Its branches curve, making the dried plant appear to be a big ball. When the wind blows, the thistle rolls along, spreading its seeds.

The First to Timbuktu

WHEN RENÉ CAILLIÉ was a young boy in France, he saw a map with a large region of Africa marked *"unknown."* He began to dream of the day when he would cross and chart the great Sahara Desert. In the early 1800s, when he was only sixteen, Caillié worked his way to the west coast of Africa, eager to begin his explorations. The French officials, however, wouldn't let him go inland. He was told that as a Christian his life would be in danger because the Moslem tribesman of the Sahara killed Christians.

Determined to have his chance, Caillié joined a nomadic Moslem tribe, claiming that he was a Moslem who had been kidnapped by the French as an infant. He was treated like a slave, but he learned the Moslem ways and something of the desert. Then he spent several years working in an indigo factory trying to earn enough money to finance an expedition into the Sahara. It was during this time that he learned the Geographical Society of Paris was offering 2,000 francs (equivalent to about $500 at that time) to the first person who could reach Timbuktu and bring back an accurate description of this city and the routes leading to it. Caillié decided to try for this prize, and on April 19, 1827, he set out.

A year and a day later, René Caillié reached Timbuktu. He soon discovered that he was not the first European to visit this city. An Englishman, Alexander Gordon Laing, had been there two years earlier. However, Laing had died before returning home, so Caillié believed he still had a chance to win the money. After carefully preparing notes about the city, he joined a caravan headed for the coast.

He was attacked and tortured by the Moslem members of the caravan. His camel was taken from him, and he was forced to walk. Caillié endured these hardships for two months because he knew he couldn't survive alone in the desert. Then, when they were closer to the coast, he left the caravan and struggled on alone, traveling only at night. Finally, René Caillié made it safely back to France. His effort was considered a triumph, and in 1828 a great reception was held to honor his accomplishment.

Dr. Livingstone, I Presume?

DR. DAVID LIVINGSTONE, an Englishman, went to Africa as a missionary in 1840. He hadn't intended to be an explorer, but his search for new mission sites repeatedly took him into uncharted territory. In 1849 he gave the first account of the Kalahari Desert. He discovered Lake Ngami and later the Zambezi River, hundreds of miles above the region where its course had previously been explored. In 1855, while navigating the Zambezi, Livingstone saw what looked like columns of smoke rising from the river and heard a constant, deep, thunderlike rumble. Livingstone discovered that what had looked like smoke was spray from a tremendous waterfall. He named it Victoria Falls, for Queen Victoria of England. News of Livingstone's explorations made him very popular with everyone back home except the missionary society. So in 1858 he left the missionary field and led an official British expedition to explore eastern and central Africa.

This trip lasted five years, and he continued to travel through the

1860s and early 1870s. His attention now focused on finding the source of the Nile River. On several occasions the world thought Livingstone was lost when attempts to reach him failed. It was during one of these times that James Gordon Bennett, Jr., manager of the *New York Herald* newspaper, launched the world-famous expedition to find Dr. David Livingstone. He sent Henry Morton Stanley, an enthusiastic foreign correspondent, to be in charge of the effort.

Stanley assembled 31 armed natives, 3 Europeans, and 153 porters to accompany him on his quest. Then he spent the next nine months trudging through the jungle. His men were weakened by disease and other hardships. He even became involved in a local war. Finally he reached the village on the shore of Lake Tanganyika where Livingstone was living.

There was a procession into the village, Stanley in the lead, followed by a man bearing the U.S. flag. His armed men fired a welcoming volley into the air as the crowd in the village parted, revealing a tall, thin, elderly white man standing alone. Stanley approached, making his now famous comment: "Dr. Livingstone, I presume?"

Unable to convince Livingstone to leave, Stanley stayed for a time. A strong friendship developed between the two men. In fact, after Livingstone died in 1873, Stanley returned to Africa to investigate the Lualaba River, which Livingstone had believed formed the headwaters of the Nile. What he actually had found was the headwaters of the Congo River. Stanley spent many years exploring Africa. In 1879 he helped to open up a new territory. This became the Congo Free State in 1908.

RIDDLE

What is dark but made from light?

A shadow.

Bug Hunt

THERE MAY NOT be any big game in your area, but wherever you live you'll find plenty of insects. To be a successful bug hunter, you'll need to build traps, set out bait, and be prepared to search for your quarry. You'll also need to decide in advance whether you'll bring the insects home alive for a bug zoo or whether you'll kill them in the field in preparation for starting a collection.

Beetle Trap

THIS TRAP is like the pits hunters have used for centuries to catch big game. Collect clean, empty tin cans with one end open. Use a garden trowel to dig a hole in the ground deep enough to sink the can so the upper edge is at ground level. If you put

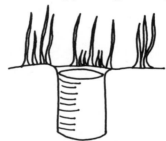

out a whole line of traps, cut wire coat hangers and tie on pieces of colored cloth to use as flags. Mark the location of each trap so you can spot it easily. To bait your trap, drop in a small piece of meat or hard-boiled egg. Check the trap each morning and again just before sundown. Some beetles are active at night. Others are active during the day.

There are approximately 20,000 different kinds of beetles in North America alone and more than 150,000 known varieties in the world. So you shouldn't have any trouble finding some. You'll know you have captured a beetle if it has a shell on its back. This shell is really the hard forewings. Underneath are membranous hind wings.

You could also look for beetles under rocks and logs or in piles of decaying leaves. If you search for beetles this way, though, leave the environment as undisturbed as possible for the plants and animals that live there.

If you're collecting beetles for your insect collection, you'll want to put them into a killing jar immediately. Have an adult prepare this for you by putting a wad of cotton into the bottom of a glass jar that has a tight-fitting lid. Then have the adult pour in enough carbon

tetrachloride (which can be purchased as a cleaning solution) to wet the cotton and place a piece of fine-mesh metal screening over this. The screen will keep insects from falling under the cotton. Keep the killing jar sealed except when you are dropping insects in or taking them out. Avoid breathing the fumes from this jar.

Take along plastic pill bottles to carry home dead beetles, and tweezers to transfer the beetles from the killing jar to the pill bottles. Jot down where you found the insect and the date on a piece of paper. Tuck this inside with the specimen. You'll need that information when you prepare your collection.

If you plan to bring your beetles back alive to investigate them close up, take along plastic containers with tight-fitting lids. Poke the lids full of tiny holes. Decide what the beetles were eating where you found them, and bring along enough of that material to provide meals during their captivity. Return these beetles to their homes after you've observed them.

Here are some beetles that you might catch.

Tiger Beetle

THIS ferocious beetle starts out life as an even fiercer larva nicknamed a doodlebug. It stands vertical in a sandy pit, and just its head and huge jaws poke out— ready to grab any insect or spider that comes within range. The more the larva eats, the bigger it gets, shedding its skin to grow. Then, after two years, it goes through a brief pupal stage and

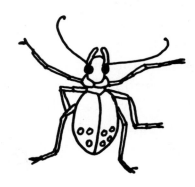

emerges as an adult. Some tiger beetles are orange and brown striped, like real tigers. Others are deep blue or shiny copper. All tiger beetles are summer prowlers, catching caterpillars, spiders, and other insects.

Stag Beetle

AS BEETLES GO, these are big bugs. Those found in North America can be as much as 2 inches (5 centimeters) long. Those that live in the tropics grow up to 4 inches (10 centimeters) long. Their huge jaws look impressive, but they aren't very effective weapons. People used to believe these beetles

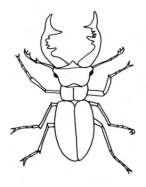

could pick up burning coals with their jaws. In reality, the males with the largest jaws are usually the weakest. Fortunately for the beetles, they don't have to fight to eat. Stag beetles eat sap, fruit, and nectar. The huge jaws are used only by males fighting for a mate.

Scarab Beetle

TO THE ANCIENT Egyptians these beetles were the symbol of new life because the adults seemed to suddenly appear from balls of dung, animal wastes. Scarab beetles are actually re-cyclers, helping to bury rot and fertilize the soil. They collect a ball of dung much bigger than they are, roll it to a safe spot, and settle down for a long meal. When the female is ready to lay her eggs, she tucks each one into a dungball. For the developing scarab beetle larva, the entire nursery is dinner.

Click Beetle

THIS FLAT, black and white beetle is most noted for the trick it uses to right itself if it lands on its back. Its legs are too short to easily push itself over. Instead, it arches its back where the stiff shell of its thorax and abdomen join, and then jerks. There is a loud click as the beetle flips in the air and lands on its feet.

Ladybird Beetle (Ladybug)

BOTH THE ADULTS and the larvae of this insect feed on aphids, scale insects, and other insects that destroy plants. Fruit growers value ladybird beetles so highly that they buy them, setting them free in their orchards.

Living Night Lights

IN TOKYO the beginning of summer is celebrated by the release of hundreds of fireflies that have been raised especially for this occasion. Also called lightning bugs, these insects are really beetles. Have you ever caught fireflies? They're easy to trap in cupped hands. Don't worry—they won't bite. Put six or more into a clear plastic or glass jar with a lid that is punched full of tiny holes. Then settle down in the dark to watch them. The fireflies produce a cool light through a special chemical reaction in their bodies.

Do all the fireflies blink in the same rhythmic pattern? Try copying the light signal of one of your trapped fireflies with a flashlight. Can you get that firefly to answer your signal? Can you attract other fireflies winging through the darkness by flashing this coded message?

You can be sure that you have a jar full of males. The females have such short wings that they can't fly. That's why fireflies do so much blinking—trying to locate a mate. So before the night's over, send your bottled fireflies on their way.

Fireflies glow throughout their lives. The tiny eggs glow as the female deposits them in soft soil. The larva that spends nearly two years growing is called a glowworm because it, too, has a tiny light on the end of its body. This light pales, though, in comparison with the flash the adult is capable of producing. In parts of India, the Philippines, and New Guinea male fireflies sometimes gather in dense swarms covering nearly every leaf of a tree. Then they flash in unison, making the tree appear to be illuminated by thousands of twinkling lights.

Stalking High Fliers

YOU'LL NEED a net to catch insects on the wing. Follow these directions to make one.
You'll need:

> a wire coat hanger
> wire cutters
> electrician's tape
> an old broom handle
> a saw
> 1 yard of mosquito netting or cheesecloth
> a strip of muslin 4.5 inches (11.4 centimeters) wide and
>   1 yard long

scissors
needle and thread
a sewing machine

(You may want an adult's help with this project.)

1. Use the wire cutters to cut the hanger on either side of the hook. Bend the wire into a loop as shown.

2. Saw the broom handle in half.

3. Place one end of the wire loop on either side of the handle and tape it securely in place with electrician's tape.

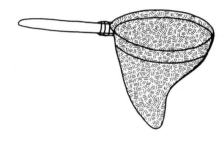

4. Fold the mosquito netting or cheesecloth in half. Trim as shown. Sew along the open edge on the sewing machine.

5. Sew the band of muslin to the top of the netting. Then fold this over the metal loop and slip-stitch to seal.

Then, as you stalk your prey, keep these pointers in mind. Always have the sun in front or to the side of you so you won't cast a shadow. You'll be more likely to find butterflies, the showiest fliers, on hot, sunny days than on cool, cloudy days. The morning after a thunderstorm is one of the peak times. Hunt in weedy thickets where milkweed, butterfly weed, or thistles are abundant. These plants attract butterflies.

To catch butterflies successfully, it helps to be a careful observer of butterfly behavior. The monarch butterfly, for example, always leaps

MILKWEED

BUTTERFLY
WEED

THISTLE

up when surprised. A regal fritillary butterfly drops to the ground when startled. Recognizing your quarry and knowing its habits can help you bag your prize. Once a flying insect is in the net, quickly twist the cloth to trap it. Always use tweezers to handle a butterfly or a moth. Your fingers will rub off some of the wing scales, making it a less attractive specimen for your collection. Transfer your catch to the killing jar.

Insect collectors usually use paper triangles to carry winged insects home. To make a paper triangle, fold one corner of a sheet of notebook paper over until the sides of the paper meet. Then fold the overlapping edges and turn down the upper corner.

Write on the outside of a paper triangle where you found the insect, the date, and, if possible, the type of plant it was on. Then tuck the insect inside, gently spreading its wings apart. A plastic or metal lunch box makes a crushproof place to file these paper triangles so you can carry them home safely.

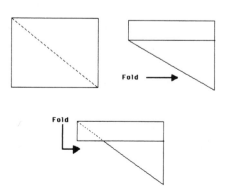

Sweet Trick

SUGARING is a way to get a variety of insects to come to you. To prepare a batch of bait, put two peeled, rotting bananas on a piece of waxed paper, mash with a fork, and fold in a fourth cup of granulated sugar. Smear this mixture on a tree trunk or a wooden fence post (check first to be sure you have permission to do this). Then settle down nearby and wait.

Light Stalker

SCOUT around porch lights or other outdoor lights at night when you're looking for night-active insects. Or you can rig a light trap. Put a lantern-style flashlight inside a white pillowcase and place this outside on the ground, spreading out the cloth. When it gets dark, switch on the light. Charmed night fliers will land on the bright cloth, and when they do, you can pounce.

A True Bug and Its Parts

YOUR SKELETON is on the inside. A grasshopper's is on the outside, like a suit of armor. As the grasshopper grows bigger, the exoskeleton splits open and the insect crawls out.

A new exoskeleton hardens on the outside of the grasshopper's now larger body. A grasshopper's body, like that of all true insects, is made up of three main parts: head, thorax, and abdomen.

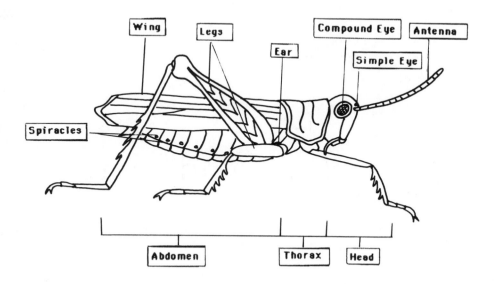

Complete Metamorphosis

METAMORPHOSIS means change. Many insects, including all butterflies and moths, go through a complete change during their lifetimes.

PUZZLER

Why did removing the old tires stacked out by the garage help get rid of mosquitoes?

(See page 112.)

PUZZLER

When are you like a butterfly?

(See page 116.)

Butterflies And Moths

CHECK OUT these differences to know whether you've captured a butterfly or a moth.

Butterfly

slender, club-ended antennae
slender body
rests with wings together
active usually in daytime

Moth

feathery antennae
fat furry body
rests with wings apart
active usually at night

Here are some butterflies and moths that you might catch.

Giant Swallowtail

WITH a wingspan of 4 to 5.5 inches (10 to 14 centimeters), this is the biggest butterfly in the United States. The adults can often be seen in the summer, gliding with outstretched wings. The females lay as many as five hundred eggs, depositing them one at a time near the tip of a leaf. The caterpillars are called orange dogs or orange puppies in the South, where they sometimes damage citrus trees.

Common Sulphur

IT'S BELIEVED that these butter-yellow butterflies and the several hundred other species of sulphurs may have been the first to be called *butter*flies. Swarms of adults can often be found gathered around a puddle or over a field of clover. You might think a female sulphur

was a different type of butterfly. Females are often a different shade or have a different-color pattern on their wings. Sulphurs are found throughout the United States but are most common in the East.

Cecropia

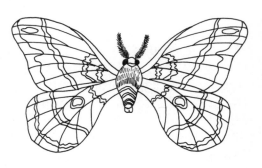

IF YOU SEE a fat, greenish caterpillar with eight rows of blue, red, and yellow bumps sticking up from its back, it's a cecropia larva. All summer long this caterpillar nibbles tree and shrub leaves, growing bigger and bigger until it's nearly 4 inches (10 centimeters) long. In the fall it spins a cocoon attached lengthwise down a twig. The adult moth that emerges in the spring is big, with a 5 to 6.5 inch (12.7 to 16.5 centimeter) wingspan. Unlike the caterpillar, it doesn't have well-developed mouth parts and never eats. It lives only long enough to reproduce. The female lays from two hundred to three hundred chalky-white oval eggs a few at a time on the underside of the leaf that will be the caterpillar's first meal. You'll find this moth from the East Coast to the Rocky Mountains.

Luna Moth

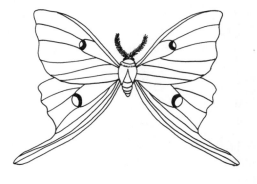

THIS BEAUTIFUL, pale green moth has long tails trailing from its hind wings. It can be found from Florida into Canada and as far west as Texas. Its caterpillars feed mainly on sweet gum, walnut, persimmon, and hickory leaves. Then they spin papery cocoons. In some parts of its range, two broods mature each year. The adults that emerge in the summer have yellow wing margins. Those that emerge in the spring have pink to purple wing margins.

Tent Caterpillar

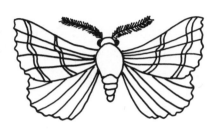

THE FAT-BODIED, hairy, brown adult moths don't do any damage, but their caterpillars are familiar tree pests. While most caterpillars live and dine alone, these larvae remain together, building a family tent of silken threads. This web is usually in the crotch of a tree. Eastern tent caterpillars prefer apple and cherry trees. The California tent caterpillars also like oak trees. The caterpillars only rest inside this web tent. They eat out, trailing a silk thread they can follow to find their way home again.

Putting Your Collection Together

BEETLES and similar insects are ready for immediate display. Butterflies, moths, and other winged insects, however, need special shaping. By the time you get them home, their wings will be too stiff to arrange without breaking. Place them—still inside their paper triangles—between two clean, damp linen towels and leave them overnight or for about twelve hours. Then move them to the setting board.

To make a setting board, first cut two pieces of ¾-inch pine 12 inches (30.5 centimeters) long and 6 inches (15 centimeters) wide. (You may want an adult's help with this project.) Sand or plane the top of each piece to slope down to the center.

Next, nail these two sloping pieces of wood to a third piece of wood—12 inches (30.5 centimeters) long and 14 inches (35.6 centimeters) wide. Leave a gap between the two sloping slats that is wider at one end than the other. The insect's body will fit down in this groove as shown in the picture. A wider space will accommodate fatter insects.

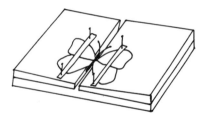

Once you've arranged the insect's wings on the setting board, hold them in place by pinning strips of paper over the wings. Use mounting pins to prepare and display the insects in your collection. These are inexpensive and available at hobby shops. Regular pins bend and rust too easily. Leave insects on the setting board for several days to be sure they are completely dry.

Display cases may be as simple as sturdy cardboard boxes—the kind sold to hold school supplies. Or you could build more elaborate wooden boxes with framed glass lids. In either case, the important thing is to prevent mold and parasites from attacking your specimens. Put mothballs in a bag and put that bag inside another bag. Hit the bag with a hammer and pour the chips into the bottom of the box.

Then top with a layer or cork, corrugated cardboard, or Styrofoam, such as the kind used for meat trays. One pin will be enough to anchor each insect. Press the pin through the thorax. Pin a label to the left and above the insect.

Each label should include the insect's scientific and common name. Books about insects will help you make correct identifications. The label should also include information about the place and the date the insect was captured. Plan to group your display in some logical way, such as putting all the beetles together and all the butterflies together. Unless specimens are carefully displayed and correctly labeled, all you have is a bunch of dead bugs.

PUZZLER

How do crickets make their chirping sound?

(See page 117.)

Weather Forecaster

WATCH for this greenish-white cricket among the leaves of trees and bushes. It's often called the temperature cricket. Supposedly, you can tell what the temperature is in degrees Fahrenheit by counting how many times it chirps in a minute, dividing by 4, and adding 40. Try it.

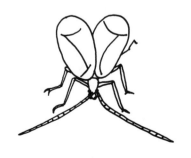

Home Sweet Hole

Y OU CAN bring an ant colony above ground, where you can watch their activities. You'll need a large glass jar that has a lid. Use a hammer and a nail to punch tiny holes in the lid. (You may want an adult's help with this.) Next, go hunting for an ant colony. You'll recognize it by the telltale mound. Use a shovel and a garden trowel to dig up soil near but not part of the colony. Crumble the dirt if it's hard, and fill the jar slightly more than half full. Then dig up the ants' current home, using the trowel to transfer the ants, any tiny white larvae you find, and, if possible, the queen. She'll be much larger than the workers. Don't worry if you don't get the queen. This will mean that the life of your colony will be limited, however. Only the queen lays eggs. Be careful—ants bite. If you live in the South or the West, where fire ants are common, use an insect book or ask an adult's help to be sure you don't choose these ants for your colony. Their bite can be particularly irritating.

Place your jar colony in a cool, shady spot and settle down to watch the workers tunneling. How do the ants carry the soil particles? What do they do with the dirt they take out of their tunnels? How do the ants clean themselves? If your colony has a queen, where is she? Where is the nursery?

Ants like moist soil, so you'll need to sprinkle on a little water once a week. Feed your ants a drop of honey, or tiny pieces of apple, banana, or walnut.

PUZZLER ANSWER

Mosquitoes go through complete metamorphosis. The female lays her eggs on the surface of any still-water pool or puddle. There the larvae, called "wrigglers," grow, and the pupae develop into adults. The old tires collected water and made a perfect mosquito breeding spot.

Hunting Wild Plants

A WEED is any uncultivated, unwanted plant, and there are weeds everywhere. Weeds are hardy and persistent—ever try to keep a garden or a yard weed-free? Some are even beautiful. So how about starting a weed collection? You'll find these wild plants in some interesting and unusual places. They grow in sidewalk cracks, along the edges of parking lots, and in dry, eroded plots.

Here are some that you might collect.

Burdock

THIS PLANT grows as much as 8 feet (2.4 meters) tall. Its seeds are inside a burr. When these burrs stick to an animal's fur coat or a person's clothing, the seeds get a free ride. Later, the burr drops off and, if the seed lands where conditions are favorable, a new Burdock plant sprouts.

Queen Anne's Lace

IT'S SOMETIMES called wild carrot. It's a member of the carrot family, and its leaves resemble those of the carrot plant. The lacy flowers are the most distinctive feature.

Sow Thistle

GROWING as much as 10 feet (3 meters) tall, this plant is prickly all over. The flowers look like pale dandelions. Other types of thistles have large purple flowers. A long taproot helps it grow even where the surface is dry.

Pokeweed

THIS WEED may tower 9 feet (2.7 meters). It has long clusters of dark reddish-purple berries. Young leafy sprouts are sometimes cooked and eaten. However, if not cooked properly, they are poisonous. The berries and roots are very poisonous.

Dandelion

YOU CAN SPOT this weed by its bright yellow flowers. When you find one, look closely at its leaves. They grow in a rosette hugging the ground. This makes the plant hard to uproot. It's even safe from slicing mower blades. Pull the dandelion gently out of the ground so you don't break its taproot. Measure the root. How long is it? Pull other dandelions and measure their roots. What is the champion root length? Why do you think this long root makes the dandelion a hardy weed?

Next, look at the stem. It's a hollow tube—a strong design for supporting a heavy flower head. Did you ever make a bracelet or a necklace by creating chains of dandelion stems? To form each link, you'll need to carefully poke one end of the stem inside the other.

Finally, examine the flower head. Dandelions belong to a plant family called composites. Every petal is actually a complete flower attached to all the parts needed to produce seeds. One dandelion flower head is capable of producing more than three hundred seeds. When it goes to seed, the flower become a ball of white fluff.

Did you ever blow on one? What happened? Try pulling a dandelion that has gone to seed apart to count how many seeds are in one flower head. How do you think dandelions are able to spread so quickly over a large area?

Some people enjoy eating dandelions. The roots can be cooked like carrots. The leaves can be eaten as a salad, and the young blossoms can be dipped in flour or a light batter and fried. If you decide to try any of these, be sure to check with an adult first and wash the dandelions carefully before eating.

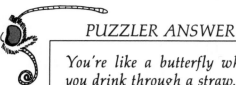

PUZZLER ANSWER

You're like a butterfly when you drink through a straw. A butterfly's mouth parts form a long tube called a proboscis, which it uses to suck nectar from flowers.

RIDDLE

What is the best day for a picnic?

ʎɐpuns ∀

Three Weeds to Avoid

L EARN to recognize poison ivy, poison oak, and poison sumac. Touching the leaves of these plants can make you break out in an itchy rash. If you think you have been in contact with one of these, wash as soon as possible with soap and water. It's the invisible oil from these plant leaves that soaks into your skin and causes the rash. You can also pick up that oil from your dog's or cat's fur if the animal has been in contact with one of those plants, or from your own clothing. This oil can even be on the towel you used when you washed up. So put soiled clothes and towels into the laundry. If you do break out in a rash, avoid scratching. This won't spread the rash, but it can open the skin, allowing an infection to start.

POISON IVY

POISON OAK

POISON SUMAC

Pressed Plants

WHEN YOU go weed hunting, take along a number of self-sealing bags, a notebook, and a pencil. You may also want an old spoon to help you dig up your specimen. Pull gently so you can get the root, too. Jot down the date and where you found your plant. Slip each plant into a separate bag.

To preserve specimens, botanists use what is called a plant press. Plants are laid between layers of paper and blotting paper. A frame of wooden slats with large open spaces is placed on the top and the bottom. Then straps pull the frame tightly against the paper. You could make a similar press or simply spread the plant on a paper towel, cover it with another, and place inside sheets of newspaper. Keep each information sheet with its plant. Then stack heavy books on top of the pile. Change the paper after two days, and again after four days. Continue to press the plants for about a week.

Mount each pressed plant on a sheet of white paper, using white glue or thin strips of adhesive tape. Use books to help you identify your plant and write both the scientific and the common name across the top of the paper. In the lower left-hand corner, list when and where you found that weed.

PUZZLER ANSWER

A chirp is produced every time a cricket closes the two hard forewings that cover the membranous hind wings. They may do this as fast as 150 times a second or as slowly as only once every three seconds. If you hear a cricket chirp, you know it's a male. Only male crickets "sing," and they do it only at night. If you live in Hawaii, you can hear a full cricket chorus. Hawaii has three times as many crickets as any other state.

A Stately Collection

YOU COULD also press and mount tree leaves. Why not try for a leaf from each of the state trees?

Alabama	*Longleaf pine*	Montana	*Ponderosa pine*
Alaska	*Sitka spruce*	Nebraska	*American elm*
Arizona	*Paloverde*	Nevada	*One-leaf piñon*
Arkansas	*Shortleaf pine*	New Hampshire	*White birch*
California	*Redwood*	New Jersey	*Northern red oak*
Colorado	*Blue spruce*	New Mexico	*Piñon*
Connecticut	*White oak*	New York	*Sugar maple*
Delaware	*American holly*	North Carolina	*Pine*
Florida	*Sabal palmetto*	North Dakota	*American elm*
Georgia	*Live oak*	Ohio	*Buckeye*
Hawaii	*Candlenut*	Oklahoma	*American redbud*
Idaho	*Western white pine*	Oregon	*Douglas fir*
Illinois	*Native oak*	Pennsylvania	*Eastern hemlock*
Indiana	*Tulip tree*	Rhode Island	*Maple*
Iowa	*Oak*	South Carolina	*Sabal palmetto*
Kansas	*Cottonwood*	South Dakota	*Black Hills spruce*
Kentucky	*Yellow poplar*	Tennessee	*Tulip tree*
Louisiana	*Bald cypress*	Texas	*Pecan*
Maine	*Eastern white pine*	Utah	*Blue spruce*
Maryland	*White oak*	Vermont	*Sugar maple*
Massachusetts	*American elm*	Virginia	*Flowering dogwood*
Michigan	*Eastern white pine*	Washington	*Western hemlock*
Minnesota	*Red pine*	West Virginia	*Sugar maple*
Mississippi	*Great-flowering magnolia*	Wisconsin	*Sugar maple*
		Wyoming	*Cottonwood*
Missouri	*Flowering dogwood*		

When you pick a leaf, be sure to take a complete leaf. Some trees have large leaves made up of a number of leaflets. To know if you have a complete leaf, look at the base of the leaf stem. If you see a bud, it's a complete leaf. If you don't see a bud, it's a leaflet.

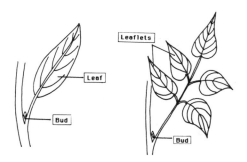

Since all these trees won't be growing in your area, plan to expand your collection anytime your family travels. You could also write to someone you know in another state, offering to trade leaves. Or you could write to the chamber of commerce in a state's capital, asking for help in locating a leaf sample.

Old Leafy

THE OLDEST resident in your neighborhood may be a tree. Look for a really big tree—most trees grow slowly so bigger means older—and try to discover its history. What kind of tree is it? When was it planted? Was it ever threatened by a flood, a fire, or a severe windstorm?

There's a really big old Moreton Bay fig tree growing in Santa Barbara, California. In 1876 the tree was only a seedling in a pot. A sailor brought it from Australia for a little girl, and in 1877 she gave it to her friend, Adeline Crabb. Adeline's mother planted the seedling in the family's back yard. Today, this tree is a giant, more than 70 feet (21 meters) tall with a trunk more than 30 feet (9 meters) around. The fig's branches spread over such a wide area that as many as fifteen thousand people could stand in its shade on a hot day. If this tree could talk, think of the stories it could tell.

On Wheels

HERE ARE some fun ways to enjoy the summer on your bicycle.

Skill Riding: Test how well you can steer and balance by setting up a special course. An empty parking lot is best for this. Save plastic milk jugs. Cut off the tops and tie a bright piece of cloth to the handle of each jug. Then fill the jugs with sand, dirt, or gravel. Place these markers about 5 feet (1.5 meters) apart in a straight line or following a zigzag path. To make the course even more challenging, mark perimeter lines with chalk, making the path about 5 feet (1.5 meters) wide. Can you maneuver the course without bumping any markers? Can you do it without going outside the boundary lines? How quickly can you successfully go from the start to the finish line?

Motocross races, also called BMX races, take place on dirt bicycle tracks ¼ mile (400 meters) long. They have bumps and sharp turns to challenge riders. Bicycles used for this kind of racing have small wheels and wide tires to prevent slipping and sliding. The cyclists wear helmets and padded clothing to protect them if they fall.

Smooth Coasting: An empty parking lot is a good place for this event, too. Use chalk to mark a starting line. Measure out 20 feet (6 meters), and draw a stopping line. When you reach this second line, stop pedaling but don't break. Coast until you can no longer stay balanced, then put your feet down. Use the kickstand to prop up your bike, and measure from the stopping line to your front tire. How far did you glide? Can you break your own record?

The Tour de France is a famous bicycle road race that is held every year with more than a hundred cyclists racing through the European countryside. The race lasts twenty-four days and covers 2,500 miles (4,000 kilometers). Bicycles built for this kind of long-distance race have lightweight frames, narrow tires, and a gear system.

Shapely Messages

BICYCLE RIDERS must obey street signs just like drivers. Some signs can be recognized at a distance by their shapes. Do you know the message that appears on each of these signs.

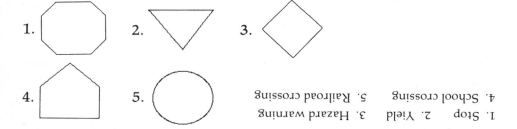

1.   2.   3.

4.   5.

1. Stop   2. Yield   3. Hazard warning   4. School crossing   5. Railroad crossing

Hand Signals

YOU WILL also need to use some signs of your own while you're riding. These are the hand signals for a right turn, a left turn, and slowing or making a stop.

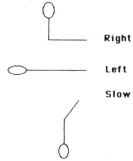

Right

Left

Slow

Hobbyhorses and Boneshakers

W HEN the first bicycle appeared in France in 1790, it didn't look at all like the bicycle you ride. It looked like a toy horse on wheels, and it was called a "hobbyhorse." There wasn't any way to steer, and the rider had to push with his feet to make the hobbyhorse go. In 1817 a forester in Germany built a bicycle by attaching two carriage wheels to a wooden frame. It still had to be pushed, but it had a steering wheel attached to the front wheel, which made it much easier to control.

In 1861 two French brothers named Michaux designed a bicycle with rotary cranks (foot pedals) attached to the front wheel. This made riding easier and faster. It also saved the cyclist's shoes. The bicycle was still made mainly of wood, however, and the wheels had iron rims. Can you imagine how hard and bumpy it must have been to ride on cobblestone streets? It's no wonder this bicycle was nicknamed "the boneshaker."

Then in 1870 an Englishman invented the Ariel, a lightweight metal bicycle with rubber tires. It had a huge front wheel about 50 inches (127 centimeters) in diameter and a little back wheel about 17 inches (43 centimeters) in diameter. Each turn of the pedal made the big wheel rotate once, so the bicycle traveled farther each time the pedals went around than it would have if the front tire were smaller. The high front wheel made bicycles so much faster, in fact, that soon bike races were being held. Racers used bigger and bigger front wheels until only the tallest men could reach the pedals.

In 1885 a young Englishman, J. K. Starley, invented what was called the "safety bicycle." This was very similar to today's bicycle. Both of the wheels were the same size, and the pedals drove the rear wheel by means of a chain and sprocket.

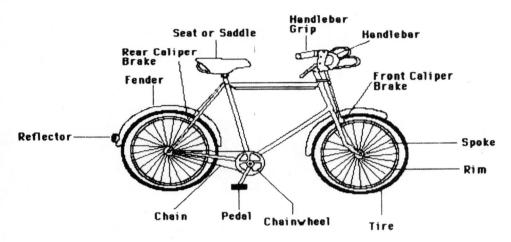

To be safe, check your bike's brakes regularly and be sure your tires have the correct air pressure. The amount of air pressure required should be marked on the side of the tire. Be sure your bike has reflectors on the front, back, and both tires. The more visible you can make yourself, the safer you'll be. If you'll be riding after dark, your bike should be equipped with a light.

Pedaling Together

THE WORLD'S longest bike was built in England in 1968. It is about 36 feet (11 meters) long and has chain 98 feet (30 meters) long. Twenty people can combine their pedaling power to make this super bike go. Wonder how it turns corners?

At the Beach

S TRETCH OUT, tummy down on a towel, and take a really close look at the sand around you. Is it made up of tiny pieces of seashells? Is it bits of crumbled rock—or maybe both? What color does the beach appear when you look out across it? Can you find different colors when you sift through a handful of sand? Start digging down. How deep do you have to go before the sand feels damp? Try packing a handful of dry sand and a handful of moist sand. Which holds its shape?

Sand Sculpture

To create sand sculptures, you'll need to move to where most of the sand is damp. Then try each of these three techniques.

1. Pack the sand into a mold, such as a plastic bucket. Then carefully dump it out. Use other molds to add onto the main shape.

2. Heap up a mound of damp sand, patting it smooth. Then use your hands, a stick, a shovel, or even a seashell to scoop and scrape away sand until the shape you want emerges.

3. Drip really wet sand, gradually building up the shape you want.

You may want to combine all three methods and add shells, feathers, stones, and other items as decoration.

If you're at the ocean, you may want to collect seashells. Here are some that you might find.

Cowry

THESE SHELLS are shiny inside and out and have "teeth" on both lips. There are many varieties of cowries. At one time these shells were used as money in Africa and the South Pacific.

Limpet

THESE LOOK like miniature volcanoes—cone-shaped with a hole at the peak. At low tide you may find the animals attached to rocks by the suction-cup action of their broad foot. Most are grayish-brown to blend with the rocks.

Queen Conch

THIS LARGE SHELL is a prize if you can find one. Between 8 and 12 inches (20 and 31 centimeters) long, it's yellowish-white on the outside and rosy pink on the inside. The shell is thick, with bumplike projections. The conch

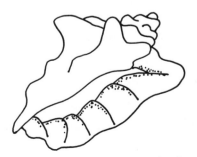

has an unusual way of moving. It pushes up, lifting its shell, and then topples over. It makes very slow but steady progress. Supposedly, if you hold a conch shell with the opening against your ear and listen, you'll hear the sound of the sea wherever you are. If you have a conch shell, try this. You'll hear a whispered roaring, but this isn't ocean noise. It's the sound of blood rushing through the vessels of your ears. The shape of the shell forms an acoustic antenna that amplifies this normally soft sound and bounces it back into your ear.

When you go shell collecting along the beach, take along two plastic buckets—one for big shells and one for small shells. Otherwise the weight of the big shells could crush tiny, delicate ones. One of the best times to shell hunt on the beach is the morning after a storm.

Use books to help you identify your shells. Egg cartons make a good display box for small shells. Or you may build a wooden box with a glass lid. The shells can be grouped by the family they belong to or by the area where they were found. Put a drop of white typewriter correction fluid on each shell, and when this is dry, write a number on it with a marking pen. Then, on a display card, list each shell's common and scientific name next to its number. Keep a file card on each shell that includes the name, where it was found, when it was found, and the shell's length.

Shell Critters

SHELLS THAT aren't collection quality can be used to create fanciful animals and useful objects. You'll need pipe cleaners and any strong adhesive cement.

To make the turtle, find a large cowry for the shell. Slip a pipe cleaner inside it, curving out the front for the neck. Stick a small cowry on the end for a head. Glue on any small, flat shells for feet, and use another pipe cleaner to attach any pointed shell for the tail. Try making a bird, a fish, or a butterfly out of shells.

Quick Sack

WHEN YOU GO EXPLORING, take along a piece of cloth about 24 inches (61 centimeters) square and two safety pins. You can fold the cloth and tuck it into a pocket or roll it up and wear it as a belt or a headband until you need it. Then follow these directions to transform the cloth into a sack:

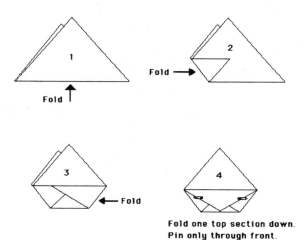

Fold one top section down.
Pin only through front.

Under the Stars

EVEN THOUGH you won't need to keep warm, there are two important reasons to have a shelter if you sleep outside in the summer—insects and rain. The Indians used to construct a one-person shelter by bending two green shoots and poking them into the ground to form an arch at either end of the shelter. Then they spread slabs of bark between these supports. A smoky fire was lit at either end to discourage mosquitoes and other flying pests. You could build an Indian-style shelter, but it kills the tree to strip off its bark. That's hardly a fair trade for a little protection.

Instead, you can carry a blanket bag, a plastic tarp (or piece of plastic sheeting) about 8 feet (2.4 meters) square, a piece of rope about 6 feet (1.8 meters) long, an old tube sock, and a piece of mosquito netting (or cheesecloth) about 4 feet (1.2 meters) square. To make the blanket bag, fold an old blanket in half and stitch the bottom and about two-thirds of the open side shut. When rain doesn't look likely, spread the plastic tarp on the ground as a moisture barrier. Then lay your blanket bag on top of this. Poke a stick into the ground at your head end, and slip the old sock over the top. This keeps the sharp wood from tearing the netting. After you crawl into the bag, drape the mosquito netting over the stick, forming a tent over your head and shoulders.

If rain is a possibility, tie the rope between two trees and drape the plastic sheet over it. Anchor the edges with stones. Then set up your blanket bag and insect netting under this shelter.

Some of the most violent storms of the year happen in the summer. Why? You'll find out and discover some special holidays that are strictly seasonal—next.

5.
STRICTLY SEASONAL

Lightning

THE PUFFY, cumulus cloud begins to billow up. The top spreads into an anvil head as the cloud thickens and darkens, becoming a cumulonimbus cloud. The wind begins to blow harder, and raindrops pelt the ground. Then, suddenly, a jagged streak of light slices across the sky. Thunder cracks explosively and trails off into a deep rumble. It's a thunderstorm, and that lightning bolt was only one of six hundred flashes that occur somewhere in the world every second. Of these, about one hundred strike the earth. Lightning is misunderstood, underrated as a dangerous phenomenon, and unappreciated for the important way it helps the environment.

People used to believe that lightning was fire bolts that gods and goddesses threw at each other. In 1752 Ben Franklin proved that lightning was electricity. He launched a kite with a metal rod at its tip into a cumulonimbus cloud. The kite string was silk, a very good conductor of electricity, and when the lightning flashed, Franklin touched the metal key tied to the string. The results were shocking. He was lucky he wasn't killed. An average bolt of lightning packs more than fifteen million volts of electricity—enough to light one million light bulbs.

Today scientists know that what happens in a cumulonimbus cloud is similar to what happens when you scuff across a wool carpet and touch something, getting a shock. You may even see a spark, a miniature lightning bolt, when this happens. All matter is made up of tiny atoms, and atoms are made up of even tinier negatively and positively charged particles. When friction knocks the negatively charged particles free, they collect on objects. Like opposite poles of a magnet, the opposite charges attract.

Strong updrafts of warm air into colder air batter water droplets, causing the cloud to become electrified. Particles with a positive charge collect in the highest layers. Negatively charged particles collect in the lower portion of the cloud. As a thunderstorm approaches, these negative charges set up an attraction with positive charges on the ground.

At first the air acts as an insulator, preventing charged particles from leaping between the earth and the cloud. Eventually the attraction becomes too great. An invisible finger of negatively charged particles shoots down from the cloud, seeking the quickest path to the ground. Then the positively charged particles leap up to meet the negative charges, forming an electrified channel that may be as thin as a wire or as thick as a cable. Lightning appears to shoot down from the sky, but slow-motion photography has proved that the bolt actually illuminates from the ground up.

All of this action lasts only a fraction of a second, but the surge of power generates a burst of heat. The explosive expansion of super-heated air creates sound waves—thunder. Since lightning travels at the speed of light—about 186,000 miles per second (300,000 kilometers per second)—and sound travels only 1 mile (1.6 kilometers) in five seconds, it really is possible to estimate how many miles (kilometers) away a storm is. Count the number of seconds between the time you see the lightning flash and when you first hear the crack of thunder. Then divide this by five. This will tell you how many miles away the storm is. Multiply the number of miles by 1.6 to find out how many kilometers this represents.

Thunderstorms happen most frequently during the spring and summer because it is then that the Earth's heat is most uneven. If you live on the island of Java, you have a lot of opportunities to practice figuring how far away the storm is. Lightning flashes there about three hundred days a year. Florida is the most lightning-prone state in the United States, averaging two thunderstorms a week.

Lightning can kill you, so if you see a developing cumulonimbus cloud, follow these lightning safety tips:

1. Never stand under a tree when there's lightning. People used to believe that some trees resisted lightning while others attracted it. (Oak courts the stroke; ash draws the flash.) All tall trees attract lightning.

2. Never be the tallest thing around. Positive charges flow over people as well as objects, and lightning seeks the quickest contact with the ground. The Empire State Building has been struck by lightning as often as nine times in a twenty-minute period.

3. Get out of the water. Water is a good conductor of electricity and lightning is electricity.

4. Don't be in contact with anything metal. Metal is also a good conductor of electricity.

5. Get inside a building or a car. Stay away from windows and doors.

Although lightning may seem to be gone in a flash, it does have an important long-lasting effect. Plants need nitrogen to grow. While there is plenty of it in the air, plants can't use it in this gaseous form. Lightning causes the gaseous nitrogen to form nitrogenous compounds that are carried to the soil by the rain. So the next time there is a thunderstorm with plenty of lightning, notice whether the grass and other plants in your neighborhood seem to have a sudden growth spurt after the storm. It isn't just the rain. The lightning provided a natural dose of fertilizer.

Weather Myths

BEFORE weather satellites and reliable forecasting, people depended on natural signs as they attempted to predict thunderstorms. Here are some of those signs and what really causes them.

Red sky at night, sailor's delight;
Red sky in the morning, sailors take warning.

A rosy red sky in the evening is caused by dry, dusty air. A red morning sky is usually caused by sunlight shining through moist air. The water vapor could become rain by afternoon.

Swallows flying low and near the ground
Means that soon a storm of rain will be found.

Insects are carried downward by cool air, and swallows follow to feed on them. This cool air could be pushing up warm, moist air, creating a cumulonimbus cloud.

A ring around the moon means rain.

People who believed this thought that a big ring meant that the storm would arrive very soon. The ring is created by moonlight shining through clouds of ice crystals. When these are low and slow-moving, the ring appears much larger than when the clouds are high and fast-moving. In 1982 the U.S. War Department Signal Service completed a six-year test that proved that this sign couldn't be counted on to predict rain no matter what size the ring.

Unlucky Seven

ROY SULLIVAN, a retired forest ranger, has been struck by lightning seven times. He's proof that it is possible to survive such shocking events. However, the lightning has singed his eyebrows, set his hair on fire, burned his shoulder, ripped off his shoe, and knocked him out of his car. It's no wonder that when storm clouds appear, people leave Roy very much alone.

Twister

WHAT CAN you accomplish in thirty seconds? A tornado can uproot trees, blow a house apart, carry away a bridge, throw cars across a parking lot, and a whole lot more. While these super storms may only affect an area as wide as a two-lane highway, wind speeds of 150 to 300 mph (241 to 483 kph) make them the most destructive storms on earth.

Usually, when a hot, moist air mass meets a cold, dry air mass, the warm air rises over the cool. Occasionally, though, the cool air settles on top, trapping the warm air. Then, if a tongue of warm air breaks through, a tunnel is formed. The warm air surges up, and the air below it rushes in to take its place. So the rapidly rising column of air becomes a funnel-shaped cloud, rotating counterclockwise with the spinning of the earth, and reaching lower and lower until it touches the ground.

The high winds knock free a lot of charged particles so that lightning constantly laces the tornado's funnel cloud. Tornadoes are also accompanied by hail. Hailstones form when raindrops are carried up into colder air until they freeze, drop—collecting another coat of water—and then are tossed back up again. If hail falls in your area, cut open one of these ice balls. (You may want an adult's help with this.) The number of rings you see tells you how many bouncing trips the hailstone made.

Tornadoes usually move from the southwest toward the northeast across the United States because this is the direction of the prevailing winds. Twisters seldom travel more than 16 miles (25.7 kilometers) before they run out of destructive energy—although one record storm that struck on May 25, 1917, started at Mattoon, Illinois and kept going until it reached the boundary of Jennings County, Indiana, 293 miles (471.4 kilometers) away. Typically, tornadoes touch down and then leap on before touching down again.

Many tornado-related deaths are caused by collapsing buildings. The rush of air into the funnel creates a partial vacuum around the tornado. The sudden removal of equalizing air pressure outside a building makes the air inside push out. The building explodes. To see how this happens, put a metal cooling rack in the bottom of an electric skillet. Set an empty plastic milk jug on this rack and pour enough water into the skillet to cover the bottom of the jug. Heat on medium for twenty minutes, adding more water as needed to keep the skillet from going dry. Then quickly put the cap on the jug and use a pot-holder to remove it from the heat.

You now have exactly the reverse of what happens to a building. The air inside the jug escaped as it was heated, and you prevented any cool air from rushing in to take its place. So there is less air inside pushing out than there is outside pushing in. As you watch, the plastic jug will slowly crumple in under the force of this greater air pressure.

Tornadoes are a worldwide wonder, but the United States has the most—more than 620 a year. The majority of these occur in what has been nicknamed "tornado alley," where warm, moist air from the Gulf of Mexico meets cold, dry Canadian air. This region includes western Texas, Oklahoma, Kansas, southern Nebraska, and Iowa.

The death toll from tornadoes has been greatly reduced since the late 1950s, thanks to weather satellites and improved radar, which make it possible to detect storms; to improved communications systems, which spread the warning to large number of people quickly; and to community preparedness, which has helped people understand how to protect themselves. The National Severe Storm Forecast Center was created in the late fifties to coordinate these efforts.

If a tornado *watch* is in effect, you should go on with what you're doing but stay tuned to your radio for updated weather reports. A watch means that conditions are right for a tornado to develop. If a tornado *alert* is issued, you should act immediately to protect yourself. An alert means that a tornado has been spotted.

What to Do If There Is a Tornado Alert

If you're walking, go inside the nearest steel and concrete building but stay away from the windows. If you can't reach a building, lie down in a ditch and cover your head.

Plan in advance where you would go at home to be safe. A basement is a good place. Or, if your house doesn't have a basement, you could go into a closet under a stairs or get under a heavy table.

If you're in a car, the driver should drive away from the storm, turning at right angles at crossroads to allow for the twister's curving path. Or you should leave the car and lie down in a ditch with your head covered.

Big Winds

THESE HUGE STORMS have winds over 100 mph (161 kph), are often hundreds of kilometers wide, and travel thousands of kilometers, causing destruction all along the way. They're called hurricanes in the United States, typhoons in China, willy-willies in Australia, baguios in the Philippine Islands, and papagallos on the west coast of Central America. They're often given other names. The people of Puerto Rico were the first to nickname these super-storms, calling them after the Saint's Day when they struck land. After World War II, meteorologists started naming the storms after wives and girlfriends. Now the official list includes masculine names as well as feminine names for the storms. Accurate tracking since 1950 has allowed people in the path of a storm to move to safety before it strikes.

RIDDLE

What rises in the morning and waves all day?

A flag.

Star Festival

THIS FESTIVAL started with a legend. According to the story, long ago, Altair, a bright star in the constellation called the Eagle, came to earth disguised as a cowherd. There he discovered the seven star sisters, whose job was to weave garments for the gods. They had come down to earth to swim. The loveliest of these maidens was Vega, the brightest star from the constellation called the Harp. As soon as Altair and Vega met, they fell in love.

The two lovers were so happy together and spent so much time together on earth that Vega completely neglected her weaving. Finally, in a rage, the heavenly mother drew her silver hairpin through the stars and created the Milky Way to separate the two lovers so they could no longer meet.

Altair and Vega grieved deeply and longed to be together. At last the Jade Emperor heard their story and decreed that for one day a year, when the two lovers' constellations were close together, they could be reunited. When that day arrived, the birds flew to the heavens and spread their wings, forming a bridge that Vega could cross to join Altair.

Tanabata, the celebration of the two lovers' day of reunion, is celebrated in Japan and China every year on July 7. In honor of the joyous occasion, people decorate bamboo branches and standards with paper chains and streamers to represent the Milky Way. They also tie poems on the branches so the breezes will carry the messages to the lovers.

On Tanabata, decorate a tree near your home with streamers and paper chains. Choose a poem or write your own and tie it to a branch. Then follow the directions below to create an origami (traditional Japanese art of paper folding) bird like the ones that bridge the Milky Way for the lovers to be together for this holiday.

Start with a square of paper. It can be any size.

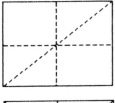

Fold along dotted lines, crease and unfold

Fold along dotted line.

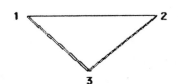

Hold at 3. Bring 2 to 3, pushing in and smoothing along the previous fold line. Repeat, bringing 1 to 3.

Bring 4 to center line. Crease and unfold. Turn over to the other side and repeat.

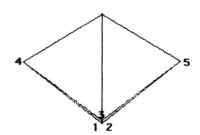

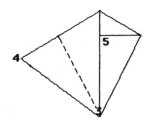

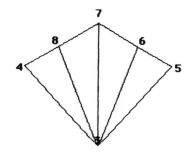

Push triangle 6,3,5 inside.
Smooth along the fold lines.

Push 8,3,4 inside and smooth.
Turn over and repeat with
the two small outer triangles
on that side.

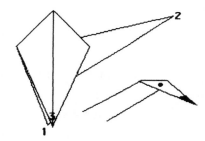

Bring point 2 up reversing
the fold. Then fold the point
down to form the head.
Color the eye and beak.
Repeat, bringing up point 1 and
reversing the fold to form the
tail.

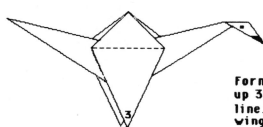

Form wing by bringing
up 3 and folding at dotted
line. Repeat with other
wing.

To make the wings flap,
gently push the tail forward
and back.

Midsummer Day

THIS HOLIDAY is celebrated on the summer solstice, June 23, when the sun barely leaves the sky. In ancient times the festivities weren't just for fun. People wanted to encourage the sun to remain high in the sky. Bonfires were lit, adding their blazing brilliance to the already bright night, and a torchlight parade was held through the fields. A wooden wheel covered with bundles of straw was set on fire to imitate the sun and sent rolling downhill. Or woven disks of twigs were lit and hurled into the sky, an early form of fireworks.

In Sweden, where it's light even at midnight on this holiday, the celebration traditionally centered around the Maj Stanger. This was a tall spruce tree that had been stripped of its branches and decorated with garlands of flowers. Sometimes it also had two hoops attached to it, possibly symbolizing the sun and the moon. The Maj Stanger recalled the ancient myth that a great tree was considered the center of creation.

Independence Day

JULY 4 is the biggest summer holiday in the United States. It commemorates the day in 1776 when the Declaration of Independence was signed. It's celebrated with parades, fireworks, and all kinds of races. Here are some events that you can enjoy with your friends.

Potato Race

MARK a starting line. Measure 50 feet (15 meters) and mark the finish line. Each racer will need a large spoon and a potato. To be fair, the potatoes should all be about the same size. Have everyone line up on the starting line, putting one hand behind his or her back and holding the potato balanced on the spoon in the other hand. At a starting signal, the race is on. If the potato drops off the spoon, it's okay to pick it up, put it back on the spoon, and go on. The first person to carry a potato across the finish line wins.

Sack Race

RACERS used to use burlap potato sacks. If you don't have any burlap bags, use large plastic garbage bags. You can use the same starting and finishing lines that were set up for the potato race or, for a greater challenge, make the race longer. Racers should line up, stepping into their sacks. It's okay to hold up the sack with one or two hands. Falls don't count if the racer can get up and go on. The first person to cross the finish line wins.

Three-Legged Race

MARK a starting line and measure 100 yards (91 meters) to a finish line. Each racer will need a partner. Standing side by side, partners loosely tie the legs that touch together. At the starting signal, the race is on. Falls don't count if the racers get up and go on. The first partners to cross the finish line win.

Wheelbarrow Race

NO, you don't need a real wheelbarrow for this race. You need a partner. Use the same starting and finishing lines set up for the three-legged race. One of the team gets down on all fours. Then the other partner picks up his or her legs at the ankles, stretching the legs out straight. At the starting signal, the racer on the ground moves forward on his or her hands. The other person follows, holding up the partner's legs. Falls won't eliminate the racers. The first partners to cross the finish line win.

A Ringing Victory

HAVE YOU EVER pitched horseshoes? This old-fashioned sport actually goes back a lot farther than you might think. It's believed to have originated in Roman army camps about 100 A.D. Although the game has been popular for centuries, particularly throughout Canada and the United States, there were no set rules until 1914.

Two, three, or four people can play. If only two or three are playing, each person competes individually. With four, players are divided into two teams. To set up a regulation horseshoe-pitching court, measure out a rectangle 50 feet (15 meters) long and 10 feet (3 meters) wide. Then set it up like the diagram below.

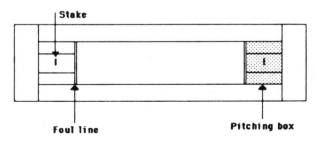

Stake

Foul line

Pitching box

You'll need to make the pitching box 6 feet (1.8 meters) square. The stake should be 1 inch (2.5 centimeters) in diameter and long enough to stand 14 inches (36 centimeters) above ground after you drive it into the center of the box. Make it tilt slightly toward the opposite stake. Spread sand, soil, or clay smoothly around the stake where the horseshoes will land.

Official horseshoes are available at sporting goods stores. A player throws two horseshoes for one turn. Pitching is done with an underhanded motion. Men pitch from 40 feet (12 meters). Women and juniors (anyone under seventeen) pitch from 30 feet (9 meters). Points are scored for the following plays:

Ringer—horseshoe encircles the stake in such a way that a line could be drawn from one tip of the shoe to the other and not touch the stake (3 points)

Leaner—horseshoe leans against the stake (1 point)

Any shoe that lands within 6 inches (15 centimeters) of the stake (1 point).

Points may be totaled by cancellation scoring or count-all scoring. In cancellation scoring, points are scored only for ringers or shoes closest to the stake that aren't tied by an opposing player. For example, if both players have a ringer, they would cancel each other out. However, if one player has a ringer and the other has a leaner, the ringer would count. In cancellation scoring, the first person to earn fifty points wins. In count-all scoring, players compete for twenty-five innings (turns), keeping track of every point they earn. The player with the highest score wins.

Fireworks

I T WOULDN'T BE the Fourth of July without these sparkling displays. Did you ever wonder how they work? Skyrockets are actually hollow paper tubes. A fuse ignites coarse gunpowder in the tail end. As hot gases escape, the rocket is launched. Just as the rocket reaches the highest point of its flight, the coarse powder ignites finer, looser gunpowder. This explodes the many small firecrackers that were packed into the skyrocket's nose. You hear loud cracks and see dazzling, starry sparkles as the gunpowder inside bursts into flame.

The different colors are produced by adding small amounts of chemicals to the gunpowder—sodium for yellow, strontium for red, copper and barium for blue and green. Charcoal may also be added. This gives the rocket a flaming tail.

In most states, it's illegal for individuals to use fireworks. Even if it is legal where you live, leave the handling of fireworks to professionals. All types of fireworks are explosive and dangerous.

Bastille Day

ON JULY 14, the French celebrate their national holiday. The people of France had been struggling to overthrow a wasteful monarchy. Finally, on July 14, 1789, they succeeded in capturing an old castle, the Bastille, which had been used as a prison. Although this was by no means the end of the war, it was a victory that rallied the people and unified their effort. Like July 4 for the United States, this date marks a turning point in history.

PUZZLER

Does the U.S. flag have more short red stripes or long red stripes? Does it have more short white stripes or long white stripes? Try to answer without looking.

(See page 150.)

Summer Stars

ONE OF the easiest constellations to spot in the summer sky is Boötes. Ursa Major and Ursa Minor, the big and little dippers, are the star bears. According to legend, Boötes was given the job of making sure these constellations didn't leave their orbit and disappear into space. Ship's captains needed to be able to sight Ursa Major and Ursa Minor to guide their ships. Boötes looks like a kite outlined by five stars. The brightest star of the constellation, Arcturus, is also one of the brightest stars in the sky. It's located at the end of the kite's tail. In June, face south, and you'll spot Boötes almost directly overhead.

The brightest star in the summer sky is Vega. Face north and look toward the east. You'll find Vega in a small constellation called Lyra, the harp. Stargazing storytellers told how Apollo, the god of sun and music, gave this harp to his favorite mortal, Orpheus. The music that Orpheus played on this harp charmed the entire universe, and Apollo was very

pleased. Then Orpheus fell in love with Eurydice and stopped playing. Angry, Apollo sent a serpent to sting Eurydice to death. Orpheus was grief-stricken, and although he played, the music was now terribly sad.

Orpheus went looking for Eurydice in the underworld, and the music he played as he searched touched the heart of Pluto, god of the underworld. Pluto promised to return Eurydice to earth if Orpheus would not look back to see if she was following him on the way to the surface. You guessed it—Orpheus looked back. Eurydice disappeared forever, and Apollo took back his lyre and hung it among the stars.

Signs of Summers Past

IF YOU FIND a tree stump, look closely at the rings. The rings formed as the tree produced xylem tissue. This tissue is made up of vascular tubes (they carry water up to the leaves and food down to be stored) and wood. Each ring is made up of lighter, less compact material produced during the spring and darker, compact material produced during the summer. Count all the dark rings. How many years old was this tree?

Thin rings show years when conditions were unfavorable for growth. Scars may also show years when forest fires raged or insects damaged the tree. If you can find out what year the tree was cut, see if you can date a summer when the tree grew slowly, indicating a drought. If possible, check old newspapers (they'll probably be on microfilm at your local library) to see if you're right.

Save It for Later

FOOD IS PLENTIFUL in the summer. However, bacteria and mold will begin to grow, and the food will spoil if it isn't preserved in some way. An early method of saving food was drying. Once the moisture was removed, bacteria and mold growth was greatly slowed. To try this, you'll need a cup of seedless grapes. Place a clean dish towel outside in a sunny spot. Spread the grapes on half the towel. Fold over the other half to cover them. This will prevent insects from landing on the fruit. Check the grapes each day. You'll know when they're dry enough. They'll look like raisins. That's what raisins are—dried grapes. Many fruits were preserved this way. Look for dried apples, prunes (dried plums), and dried apricots at the grocery store. Today, foods are dried in special ovens.

Many foods are also canned and frozen to preserve them. Food that is canned is heated to a very high temperature—hot enough to kill any mold or bacteria. Then it's sealed. What foods does your family regularly eat that come in cans? To see how well freezing preserves food, place a slice of bread uncovered on a piece of plastic wrap in the freezer section of your refrigerator. Place a second slice uncovered on a piece of plastic wrap on the kitchen counter. Check both slices every day. How long is it before you see mold appear on the unfrozen slice? Check for an additional week. Any signs of mold on the frozen slice?

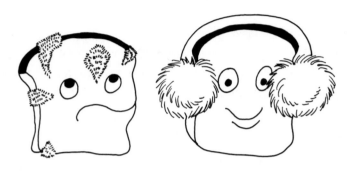

PUZZLER ANSWER

There are more short red stripes (four) than long ones (three) on the U.S. flag. However, there are an equal number of short and long white stripes.

RIDDLE

With what vegetable do you throw away the outside, cook the inside, eat the outside, and throw away the inside?

Corn on the cob.

Stop! Look, Listen, and Sniff Summer

SUMMER is such an action-packed time that you may be too busy to notice some of the season's special features. Take a few minutes on a warm, sunny day to sit quietly and observe. Look all around you. Do you see any ants at work? Is there a fat caterpillar chewing on a leaf? Don't think you were lucky to catch that young insect during its dinnertime. Caterpillars are nonstop eaters. Are there any bees or butterflies sipping nectar? What birds can you spot? Do any of them have a nest nearby? If you can see any people, what are they doing? Are any of these strictly summertime activities?

Next, close your eyes and listen. What sounds are clues to things going on close to you that you hadn't noticed before? Listen harder. Are there soft, distant sounds that let you know what's going on farther away than you could possibly see? Can you identify any sounds that are unique to summer—the noise of air conditioners running, the ice cream truck's music, kids splashing in a pool?

Finally, with your eyes still closed, inhale deeply. What does summer smell like? Is it dusty? Is there the sweet aroma of flowers? Maybe if it's very hot and you're sweaty, you can even smell yourself.

You've discovered that it's a lot of fun to explore outside in summer, but sometimes even summer weather can be terrible. What can you do when it's pouring down rain? And what about those days when it's just too hot to be outside? Well, when summer is too awful to go outside, stay inside and explore the next chapter.

6.
UNDERCOVER
INVESTI-
GATIONS

Color It Cabbage

IN THE DAYS when people not only made all their own clothes but even spun the yarn and wove the material, they used natural dyes. During the summer, wildflowers, bark, berries, and even certain clays were collected, and batches of dye were cooked up outside in big kettles. Iron pots were used for dark colors. Copper kettles were used for bright colors. When the weather's nice, you could collect some of these wild dye materials or experiment with others that you find. Try goldenrod (the whole plant or just the flowers), pine needles, dandelion roots, pokeweed berries, strawberries, and walnut husks (be careful—these will stain your skin, too). Or try these items that you can find around the house or at your local grocery store: purple cabbage (shades of lavender), onion skins (pale yellowish), and tea (brown). Then use them to make a natural dye sampler or to tie-dye a T-shirt when you need to stay indoors. (You may want an adult's help with this project.)

To prepare the dyes, you'll need three one-pound-size, clean metal coffee cans. Place these in an electric skillet and pour enough water around them to cover the bottoms of the cans. Add a cup of chopped dark outer cabbage leaves to the first can, a cup of chopped papery onion skins to the second can, and six tea bags to the third can. Add enough water to fill each can two-thirds full. Then heat the skillet on medium-high and keep adding water around the cans as needed to keep the skillet from going dry.

You can use 3-inch (7.6-centimeter) squares of 100 percent white wool or 100 percent white cotton for the sampler and a 100 percent cotton T-shirt for the tie-dyeing. Do not use any synthetic fibers or cloth that has been treated in a special way because these will not easily accept the dyes. *Scouring* is the term used to describe washing the cloth before beginning the dyeing process. To scour the cloth, soak it in hot, soapy water overnight. Rinse well and squeeze out any excess water.

To help the dye penetrate the fibers, the cloth should also be *mordanted*. To do that, dissolve 1 ounce (28.3 grams) of alum and ¼ ounce (7 grams) of cream of tartar in 1 cup of hot water. Pour this into a large kettle and add 4 quarts (3.8 liters) of water and the scoured material. Simmer for one hour.

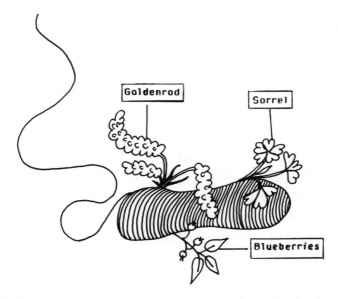

To dye the sampler squares, simply put each cloth into the dye batch of your choice. Simmer for thirty minutes. Then set a metal cooling rack over waxed paper and spread the squares on it. After they're dried, mount them on a piece of poster board, labeling what dye material was used to color each square.

To tie-dye a T-shirt, first gather the front of the shirt into knots and secure these with rubber bands. Next, dip a complete knot into a dye and let it soak and simmer for thirty minutes. Take out the knot and let it dry. After each of the knots has been colored, repeat this process, dyeing just the end of the knot with another color. For best results, use a lighter color for the whole knot and a darker color for the tip. Let the T-shirt completely dry before you undo the knots.

PUZZLER

Spider webs trap insects because the strands are sticky. An insect that lands on the web is stuck. So how do spiders keep footloose running around on their own web threads?

(See page 159.)

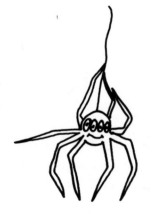

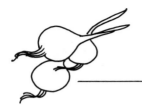

Vegetable Notes

LOOK THROUGH the refrigerator for any vegetables that might make interesting prints. Green-pepper slices are particularly nice. You could try onions, corn on the cob, zucchini squash, and even snap beans. You'll want to avoid anything that is soft and juicy. Be sure to check for permission before you start printing. Spread out newspaper to protect your work area. Use acrylics or tempera paint and plain typing paper. You may want to fold or trim the paper to note size before you start. To print, hold onto the vegetable, touch the lower surface to the paint, and press it onto the paper. You may want to use a single vegetable printed in several different colors or make a collage of different vegetable prints.

Texture Hunters

COLLECT textures of all kinds by placing a piece of white paper over an object and rubbing with the broad side of a crayon. Then cut out a square of the texture rubbing, glue it onto an index card, and print a clue about the mystery object on the back. For example, a clue for a texture rubbing of a window screen could be "air sieve." Number the cards and keep a master list so you'll know what object produced each rubbing. Then invite some friends to try to track down the mystery objects.

Finger Weaving

WHEN YOU have time on your hands, why not put your fingers to work, weaving? All you need to whip up a terrific belt or headband is a skein of yarn in your favorite color. Varicolored yarn gives a rainbow effect.

First, tie a loop of yarn around one thumb—your left if you're right-handed or vice versa. Bring the yarn behind your index finger, around the palm side of your middle finger, behind your ring finger, and on the palm side of your little finger. Then bring the yarn completely around your pinky and wind it back to your index finger in the reverse pattern. Repeat this complete set of loops a second time. There will now be two loops on each finger, and the yarn will go off from the palm side of your index finger.

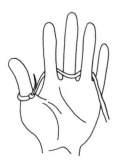 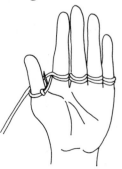

Pull on the free end of the yarn to be sure the loops are snug. Then, beginning with your little finger, slip the bottom loop over the top loop and over your finger. Repeat this process with each finger, pulling the free end of the yarn to tighten the loops each time.

Finally, start the cycle over again, bringing the free end of the yarn from the back of the index finger to the palm side of the middle finger, to the back of the ring finger, and so forth. There must be two loops on each finger each time you're ready to slip the bottom loop over the top.

When the strip you're weaving is as long as you want it, carefully slip the final loops off your fingers. Then run a short piece of yarn through these loops, and tie it in a knot. This prevents your weaving from pulling apart.

Hold That Page

YOU CAN USE some of the flowers you collected and pressed to make a bookmark. Use only really flat flowers and leaves. Cut two rectangles of clear contact paper 2 inches (5 centimeters) wide and 6 inches (15 centimeters) long. Peel the paper off one piece and arrange your flowers on the sticky side. Peel the paper off the other piece and press the sticky side down over the flowers. Finally, use a hole punch to make a hole near the center bottom. Thread a piece of colored yarn or ribbon through this hole, tie a knot, and let the ends dangle.

Finjan

THIS IS a popular game that the Bedouins (nomadic people who live in the desert regions of the Arabian peninsula and North Africa) enjoy. Two or more people may play. With more than two, divide into two teams. You'll need a tray, nine cups, and a ring (use the pop top from a soft drink can) or a small stone. This game is also played with twelve cups for a longer version. To play, first one team takes the tray with the cups somewhere where no one else can see. They turn all the cups upside down and hide the ring or stone under one cup. When they return to the playing area, the other team takes turns guessing which cup hides the prize. If their first guess is correct, they earn nine points (or twelve if twelve cups are used). The number of points to be earned decreases by one with each guess. When there are only two cups left, a wrong guess equals a loss—zero points. Then the other team goes off to hide the ring or stone.

Miniature Planetariums

YOU DON'T have to go outside to see the stars. You don't even have to wait until night. You can build your own star projector to display the constellations. You'll need a potato chip can—the kind that is a cardboard tube with a plastic lid.

PUZZLER

> *How do flies walk upside down on the ceiling without falling off?*
> *(See page 162.)*

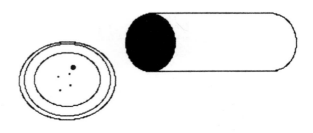

Use a knife to cut off the closed end of the can. (You may want an adult's help with this.) Next, use sharp scissors to cut a circle out of the plastic lid. Cut poster board disks that are a little smaller than the inside of this lid. Then, one at a time, put the disks on a stack of old magazines and use a needle to poke holes—one for each star—in the pattern of a familiar summertime constellation. Use books and star maps to help you design your star disks. Wiggle the needle to make the holes a little larger than pinpoints. Enlarge holes representing brighter stars even more. Label the name of the constellation on the disk.

To view the stars, go into a darkened room. Place a disk in the plastic lid and put the lid on the end of the cardborad tube. Then switch on a flashlight and push the lighted end up into the tube. Aim your star projector at the ceiling or any plain surface.

PUZZLER ANSWER

Flies are able to walk upside down without falling because their feet have sticky pads with tiny ridges. These special foot pads act like suction cups.

Summer All Winter Long

YOU CAN bring a little of the outdoors inside to create a terrarium, a glass-enclosed miniature garden. Dr. Nathaniel Ward, a London physician, built the first terrarium in the summer of 1829. It was actually a delightful accident. Dr. Ward wanted to watch an adult sphinx moth emerge from its cocoon. So he scooped garden soil into a glass container, buried the cocoon in the dirt, and sealed the top so the moth couldn't escape. To his surprise, the seeds and spores in the soil sprouted and flourished without ventilation or watering. In fact, the plants thrived for four years. Dr. Ward experimented with larger containers, and as word of his discovery spread, so did the popularity of what were called Wardian cases. True Wardian cases are a separate world—tightly sealed. They were perfect for Victorian homes, which were often very cool and dimly lit. Although the terrarium you'll create will need very little attention, it won't be permanently sealed. Today, with central heating and artificial lights, the terrarium's environment will need a little regulating from time to time.

The first step is to choose a clear glass or plastic container. An aquarium is ideal, but you could also use a glass cookie jar or a plastic storage cube. Cover the bottom with a layer of small pebbles that you've collected and washed. Or use a layer of perlite (obsidian rock that has exploded into a white granular material because it was subjected to intense heat) about 1 to 2 inches (2.5 to 5 centimeters) deep.

Next, plan the landscape for your tiny world. If space allows, include a hill and a lower area. Use rocks you've collected while you were exploring to add interesting "outcrops" and "cliffs." Put tap water in a bucket and rinse these rocks thoroughly before using them. Then prepare a batch of soil, following one of these two recipes:

NATURAL SOIL

1. Use garden or forest soil, but first spread it in a metal cake pan and bake it at 180°F (82.22°C) for one hour to kill any insect pests or fungi that are present.
2. Then mix together equal parts of soil, sand (not seashore sand), and peat moss.
3. Add a tablespoon of crushed eggshells for every 1 quart (1 liter) of soil mixture.

SPECIAL BLEND

1. Mix together equal parts of peat moss, perlite, and vermiculite (mica that has been subjected to extremely high temperatures).
2. For every 1 quart (1 liter), add 1 tablespoon of crushed eggshells.

One of the nice things about a terrarium is that it doesn't have to be watered—a sealed terrarium may not need watering for years. As a separate world, it has its own water cycle. Moisture from the soil and the plants evaporates, creating a very humid atmosphere. As the air inside the terrarium cools, this moisture condenses, returning water to the soil, where it can be collected by the plants' roots. To supply the initial water to start the cycle in your terrarium, you need to moisten the soil. Put the soil that you've prepared in a bucket and begin stirring in water one-fourth cup at a time. Mix well after each addition and stick your finger down into the soil to test it. When you first feel moisture, stop. Transfer the soil to the terrarium by the handful rather than dumping it in. This helps keep the soil from packing down. Reserve some to sprinkle around the plants, helping to blend them into the environment.

Choose plants for your terrarium that have similar requirements for sunlight, temperature, and water. You may purchase your plants, but to create a terrarium that is really like a bit of the summertime outdoors, dig up your own. Be sure you have permission before you go digging. Pick small plants because they'll look better in your little world. You can keep the plants in small pots until you're ready to create your terrarium. You may even want to leave the plants in their pots, digging these into the soil. This will slow down growth and keep you from having to trim or replant the terrarium for some time. Be creative as you landscape your terrarium world.

Put on the cover and for the first few days observe the terrarium closely. If you have overwatered, large droplets will form on the lid and drip down. Too much moisture encourages mold growth and rots roots. Leave the terrarium uncovered for several hours to allow it to dry out somewhat. If you have underwatered, you won't see the sides mist over at all. Open the lid and sprinkle on one-fourth cup more water.

Never put your terrarium in direct sunlight. Too much heat will build up. How much light your terrarium requires will, of course, depend on the plants you chose. Watch for yellow leaves. This may indicate that the plants aren't receiving enough light. If you need to use artificial lighting, fluorescent lights are best because they give off very little heat. Never leave plants in continual "daylight." While they're receiving light, green plants are busy producing food through photosynthesis. (For more information see page 28.) Most green plants need about eight hours of darkness every twenty-four hours to rest.

The End *(for this year)*

ONCE THE DAYS begin to be noticeably shorter, summer is over. Migrating birds will head for their winter homes. Flowers that have bloomed all summer long will fade—although weeds won't give up until after the first hard frost. It will start to feel cool even before sunset. Oh, there will probably still be a few summery-hot days, but these won't last long. In northern regions, leaves are changing from green to scarlet, rust, and gold. Caterpillars are wrapping up in cocoons. Hibernating animals are finding a late snack and looking for shelter. Earthworms are digging deep down—below where the icy fingers of frost can reach.

There will be a lot of new things for you to do, but summer exploring—that warm, action-packed fun—is over.

You'll have to wait until the next time it's summer to try those sunny investigations and go summer-exploring again.

INDEX